EPHESIANS:
DISPENSATIONALLY CONSIDERED

A GRACE EXPOSITIONAL COMMENTARY

SECOND EDITION

Dr. David Alan Greene

GraceWord Publishing, LLC
www.gracewordpublishing.com
U.S.A.

GRACEWORD PUBLISHING

Contents

To My Daughter, Darlena

May the eyes of your understanding be enlightened;
May you know what is the hope of *His Calling*.
May you understand the riches of the glory
of His inheritance in the saints.
May you see the exceeding greatness of His power
towards them who believe.

Acknowledgements

To my fellow grace believers, I am grateful for your words of encouragement. There are too many to list by name, but you know who you are. There are a few individuals who worked with me during the editing process. I owe a special thanks to Winnie Stearns and Frances Greene who assisted me in proofreading the text.

Introduction

Before we begin our study of the book of Ephesians, some readers may need me to cover some preliminary ground. The letter to the Ephesians is one of thirteen epistles written by Paul. Each was written to a group of believers or an individual such as Titus and Timothy. All of them, except for the letter to the Romans, were written to people Paul had visited personally. He had lived with them and taught them face to face. Therefore, the recipients of these letters had a general understanding of Paul's doctrines before receiving their letter. This may leave you, the reader, at a disadvantage if your exposure to Pauline teachings are limited.

Paul continued his relationship with those he had taught the Gospel of Grace. This gospel message must not be confused with the Gospel of the Kingdom. The letter to those in Rome was different than the others and, for that reason, it is placed first in the series of his epistles. Some of those who had heard Paul teach relocated to the capitol city of Rome.

Many there had not met or heard Paul teach and became believers indirectly through the testimony of others. It is for that reason that the epistle to those in Rome is the definitive book—a summary of Paul's teachings or doctrine. It was written to provide a comprehensive foundation of doctrine and, upon which, all his other letters were written.

Picture a multi-part series of an epic story like Star Wars. Think how difficult it would be to understand the full extent of the story in the middle. It is for this reason that I am providing a summary of the earth-shaking revelation taught by Paul. He made three missionary trips, and his last trip would be to Rome and there he would be executed. He wrote this letter to those in Ephesus while he was a prisoner in Rome awaiting his trial. He was familiar with many of them because he had taught them face to face.

As an apostle, Paul was given a unique gospel message by the Risen Savior which had remained a mystery until it was disclosed to him. That gospel message was specifically directed to the Gentiles. God states this fact. God told Ananias to heal Paul's blindness which resulted from his confrontation with the Risen Savior on the Road to Damascus. Acts 9:3-9:

3 And as he journeyed, he came near Damascus: and suddenly there shined round about him a light from heaven:
4 And he fell to the earth, and heard a voice saying unto him, Saul, Saul, why persecutest thou me? 5 And he said, Who art thou, Lord? And the Lord said, I am Jesus whom thou persecutest: it is hard for thee to kick against the pricks.

6 And he trembling and astonished said, Lord, what wilt thou have me to do? And the Lord said unto him, Arise, and go into the city, and it shall be told thee what thou must do. 7 And the men which journeyed with him stood speechless, hearing a voice, but seeing no man. 8 And Saul arose from the earth; and when his eyes were opened, he saw no man: but they led him by the hand, and brought him into Damascus. 9 And he was three days without sight, and neither did eat nor drink.

Paul had never met Jesus during His earthly ministry. Therefore, he could not have fulfilled the requirements for the replacement of Judas as the twelfth apostle (*cf.* Acts 1:21-26).

We need to pay close attention to the dialogue between God and Ananias. Acts 9:10-16:

> 10 And there was a certain disciple at Damascus, named Ananias; and to him said the Lord in a vision, Ananias. And he said, Behold, I am here, Lord. 11 And the Lord said unto him, Arise, and go into the street which is called Straight, and enquire in the house of Judas for one called Saul, of Tarsus: for, behold, he prayeth, 12 And hath seen in a vision a man named Ananias coming in, and putting his hand on him, that he might receive his sight.

> 13 Then Ananias answered, Lord, I have heard by many of this man, how much evil he hath done to thy saints at Jerusalem: 14 And here he hath authority from the chief priests to bind all that call on thy name. 15 But the Lord said unto him, Go thy way: for he is a chosen vessel unto me, to bear my name before the Gentiles, and kings, and the children of Israel: 16 For I will shew him how great things he must suffer for my name's sake.

In his letter to the Galatians, another of Paul's epistles, he explains to them something he most likely shared with the Ephesians while he was with them in person. The verses below concern his second meeting with the other apostles in Jerusalem. He only met Peter and James once before on his previous trip. Galatians 2:1-9

1 **Then fourteen years after I went up again to Jerusalem with Barnabas, and took Titus with me also. 2 And I went up by revelation, and communicated unto them that gospel which I preach among the Gentiles, but privately to them which were of reputation, lest by any means I should run, or had run, in vain.**

3 **But neither Titus, who was with me, being a Greek, was compelled to be circumcised: 4 And that because of false brethren unawares brought in, who came in privily to spy out our liberty which we have in Christ Jesus, that they might bring us into bondage: 5 To whom we gave place by subjection, no, not for an hour; that the truth of the gospel might continue with you.**

6 **But of these who seemed to be some-**

what [of importance], (whatsoever they were, it maketh no matter to me: God accepteth no man's person:) for they who seemed to be somewhat in conference added nothing to me:

7 But contrariwise, when they saw that <u>the gospel of the uncircumcision</u> was committed unto me, as <u>the gospel of the circumcision</u> was unto Peter; 8 (For he that wrought effectually in Peter to the apostleship of the circumcision, the same was mighty in me toward the Gentiles:)

9 And when James, Cephas, and John, who seemed to be pillars, perceived the grace that was given unto me, they gave to me and Barnabas the right hands of fellowship; that <u>we should go unto the heathen,</u> and <u>they unto the circumcision.</u>

This meeting took place prior to his writing to the Ephesians while he awaited his trial in Rome.

Paul provides a very conctiise statement of the Gospel of Grace. Notice his use of the definite article "the" when referring to his gospel. The definite article means it is singular and unique. Corinthians 15:1-4:

> 1 **Moreover, brethren, I declare unto you <u>the gospel</u> which I preached unto you, which also ye have received, and wherein ye stand; 2 By which also ye are saved, if ye keep in memory what I preached unto you, unless ye have believed in vain.**

> 3 <u>**For I delivered unto you first of all that which I also received,**</u> **[1] how that Christ died for our sins according to the scriptures; 4 [2] And that he was buried, and [3] that he rose again the third day according to the scriptures:**

See the simplicity of the Gospel of Grace. The gospel consisted of Christ's death on the Cross, His burial, and His resurrection. Believing is everything we need for our salvation. Jesus Christ accomplished it all for us leaving nothing else for us to do.

Paul makes it clear — the sufficiency of Christ's completed work on the Cross. He does this by reminding them that nothing else can be added. This is perhaps one of the most quoted of Paul's verses. Ephesians 2:8-9:

8 For by grace are ye saved through faith; and that not of yourselves: it is the gift of God: 9 Not of works, lest any man should boast.

In Galatians he chastised some for adding works as a requirement for salvation in addition to what the Savior had already done. Many still do this today!

Paul's gospel message is different from that of the Twelve. In Galatians 1, he affirms that he did not receive it from the other apostles or from anyone else. He received it directly from the Risen Savior. Galatians 1:11-12:

11 But I certify you, brethren, that the gospel which was preached of me is not after man. 12 For I neither received it of man, neither was I taught it, but by the revelation of Jesus Christ.

Why Paul? I asked my Methodist pastor, when I was growing up, why he did not preach from Paul's letters. He told me that it was because Paul had persecuted the Church, therefore, he shunned him. Here is Paul's view on that. Verses 13-17:

13 For ye have heard of my conversation [lifestyle] in time past in the Jews' reli-

gion, how that beyond measure I persecuted the church of God, and wasted it:
14 And profited in the Jews' religion
above many my equals in mine own nation, being more exceedingly zealous of
the traditions of my fathers.

15 But when it pleased God, who separated me from my mother's womb, and
called me by his grace, 16 To reveal his
Son in [to] me, that I might preach him
among the heathen[Gentiles]; immediately I conferred not with flesh and
blood [any man]:

17 Neither went I up to Jerusalem to
them which were apostles before me;
but [instead] I went into Arabia, and
[later] returned again unto Damascus.

God set a part Paul for a special ministry to the
Gentiles. That did not mean that the offer of the Gospel of Grace was not also open to the Jews. It is available to everyone but effective for only those who believe. Paul refers to this throughout this and other
epistles.

There is one last point I would like to make.
This will help those new to this whole concept that

Paul is different from the other writers of Scripture. Find a large jumbo paper clip. Beginning with the last page of Acts and ending with the first page of Hebrews place the paper clip over the pages in between. The books contained within the paper clip should start with Romans and end with Philemon. These are the thirteen epistles written by Paul.

In the last chapter of Acts, immediately before Paul's first book, there is a meeting recorded. It happened while Paul was incarcerated in Rome. He called the local Jewish leaders to meet with him (*cf.* Acts 28:16-30). After reasoning with them at great length, they left debating among themselves. Paul makes a proclamation. It is recorded in Acts 28:28:

28 Be it known therefore unto you, that the salvation of God is sent unto the Gentiles, and that they will hear it.

So ends the portion of Scripture which precedes Paul's epistles. Now, let's look at the other side.

If you turn to the portion of Scripture which follows Paul's epistles, the first book you come to is Hebrews. Are you seeing a pattern here? The message Paul would carry was to the Gentiles and was called the Gospel of Grace. Grace means gift. Having faith means believing what someone said. So, salvation from this message means believing that God is graciously offering salvation as a gift to anyone who will believe. Christ paid the price in full!

I would like you to see something else before we move on. There is another book that follows Paul's letters. I was teaching a Bible study and explaining salvation by grace through faith when someone interrupted me. "Hey, what about 'faith without works is dead'?" He was speaking about the verses in James. So, we all turned and read the verses in James 2:18-20:

> 18 **Yea, a man may say, Thou hast faith, and I have works: shew me thy faith without thy works, and I will shew thee my faith by my works.**
>
> 19 **Thou believest that there is one God; thou doest well: the devils also believe, and tremble.** 20 **But wilt thou know, O vain man, that <u>faith without works is dead</u>?**

He confirmed these were the verses of which he was speaking. Then, I directed them to the beginning of the book of James. I read aloud the salutation from verse 1:

1 **James, a servant of God and of the Lord Jesus Christ, to the twelve tribes which are scattered abroad, greeting.**

James is writing to the twelve tribes scattered abroad. I asked him which tribe he was from. In other words, James is writing to the children of Israel scattered amongst the nations. All the books following Paul's epistles, from Hebrews to Revelation, are written to Israel; not the Gentiles.

GraceWord Publishing has excellent books explaining this division in greater detail. My book entitled Letters to Theophilus is a summary of the Bible from Genesis to Revelation. It is a great book for understanding the framework of the Bible. There are also other online resources. I was first introduced to rightly dividing by watching online YouTube and television shows of by Les Feldick, a mid-west rancher who has taught many. He is with the Lord now, but his video classes are excellent.

Now, with this brief introduction to Paul and his unique gospel message, we are ready to begin our study of the book of Ephesians.

1

The Great City Of Ephesus

When interpreting Scripture, it is important to do so within its historical context. The geographic and political setting has an affect on both the writer and those to whom the original letter was written. It is best understood when seeing it through their eyes. Therefore, let us enter the world of first century Ephesus, a thriving regional metropolis of the Roman Empire.

The ancient city of Ephesus is in Asia Minor, current day Turkey. It was located on the coast and received caravans of traders along the coastal highways along with ships since it was a major seaport. Located on the Mediterranean Sea, it had ships arriving with imports as well as exporting with its own regional products to distant parts of the Empire. Some of these regional products included marble, wine, wool, and grain. They would expedite shipments throughout the Empire. These imported products included beef, corn, glassware, iron, lead, leather, olive oil, perfumes, purple dye, silk, silver, spices, timber, and tin. It was also a hub of transportation for passengers including Roman troops.

Ephesus was located at the crossroads of land and sea routes linking the Empire. At the time of this printing, there is an excellent map of Roman Trade routes located on the internet. We were unable to obtain information about its owner. Since this is an illustration worth studying, the map can be viewed by use of this barcode or URL:

https://4.bp.blogspot.com/-w5PitU-oOIVg/WIYAxyLKY8I/AAAAAAAA--k/eOKLLVDs2OAYwZFzYXTY_lGAZZSjnm9sgCLcB/s1600/Roman_Empire.jpg

The prominence of Ephesus for Roman commerce led to its diversity of cultures. This included religious and cultic influences. Within this city was located the great temple of the Roman goddess Diana, known by her Greek name as Artemis. Her influence cannot be understated. Other countries knew her by the names of Ishtar, Astarte, Semiramis, and Inana. Here is a link to a picture of this temple on the internet along with its URL:

 https://www.lookan-dlearn.com/history-im-ages/pre-view/A/A824/A824740.jpg

In the book of Acts, Paul's teaching causes a confrontation with the artisans whose income is derived by selling silver charms of this goddess. His teaching was having a negative impact on their livelihood. You can read about the uproar in Acts 19:22-41. It is the story about a clash between the people of God and those who choose to seek after other gods. Here are the highlights. Acts 19:23-26:

> 23 **And the same time there arose no small stir about that way. 24 For a certain man named Demetrius, a silversmith, which made silver shrines for Diana, brought no small gain unto the craftsmen;**
>
> 25 **Whom he called together with the workmen of like occupation, and said,**

Sirs, ye know that by this craft we have our wealth. 26 Moreover ye see and hear, that not alone at Ephesus, but almost throughout all Asia, this Paul hath persuaded and turned away much people, saying that they be no gods, which are made with hands:

It appears the dispute was over the worship of the goddess Diana, but it was more than that. Great fortunes were made and continue to be made from religion. Verses 27-28:

27 So that not only this our craft is in danger to be set at nought; but also that the temple of the great goddess Diana should be despised, and her magnificence should be destroyed, whom all Asia and the world worshippeth.

28 And when they heard these sayings, they were full of wrath, and cried out, saying, Great is Diana of the Ephesians.

As with any confrontation of the established norm, it was not difficult to form a crowd. Many were swept along with the crowd simply out of curiosity. The above portion of the story was included to give you a sense of the intense passion in which this predominant religion held sway in Ephesus. It is the same with the present-day culture who reject biblical truth. Ephesus was not unlike other cities of that time. The population, if not Jewish, was pagan and given over to the worship of idols and false gods. A similar story occurs in the City of Athens, another great Roman city at that time.

The following is the story of the UNKNOWN GOD. It is recorded for us by Luke in Acts 17 and reveals the pervasiveness of superstition in this pagan culture. This pagan culture is that of the Gentiles. It is to this group of pagans, the uncircumcised, the Apostle to the Gentiles was sent. Acts 17:22-31:

> 22 Then Paul stood in the midst of Mars' hill, and said, Ye men of Athens, I perceive that in all things ye are too superstitious. 23 For as I passed by, and beheld your devotions, I found an altar with this inscription, TO THE UNKNOWN GOD. Whom therefore ye ignorantly worship, him declare I unto you.
>
> 24 [He is the] God that made the world and all things therein, seeing that he is Lord of heaven and earth, dwelleth not in temples made with hands;

25 Neither is worshipped with men's hands, as though he needed any thing, seeing he giveth to all life, and breath, and all things;

26 And hath made of one blood all nations of men for to dwell on all the face of the earth, and hath determined the times before appointed, and the bounds of their habitation; 27 That they should seek the Lord, if haply they might feel after him, and find him, though he be not far from every one of us: 28 For in him we live, and move, and have our being; as certain also of your own poets have said, For we are also his offspring.

29 Forasmuch then as we are the offspring of God, we ought not to think that the Godhead is like unto gold, or silver, or stone, graven by art and man's device.

30 And the times of this ignorance God winked at; but now commandeth all men every where to repent: 31 Because he hath appointed a day, in the which he will judge the world in righteousness by that man whom he hath ordain-

ed; whereof he hath given assurance unto all men, in that he hath raised him from the dead.

Notice the Jewish leaders' response of indifference in verses 32-33:

32 And when they heard of the resurrection of the dead, some mocked: and others said, We will hear thee again of this matter. 33 So Paul departed from among them.

It is to this challenging field of ministry that the Apostle Paul was sent—to proclaim the Gospel of Grace to the Gentiles and to any who would listen. This is not much unlike our own culture with its own set of unique challenges!

2

Ephesians 1 (Part I)

Paul opens his letter with his personal greeting. He makes clear from the beginning his unique position as an *apostle*. An *apostle* is an appointed position and given by God. An apostle is a messenger or delegate who carries a message from the One who makes the appointment. Paul was appointed by Jesus Christ by the will and approval of God.

Paul is writing to grace believers in Ephesus and its surrounding area. Copies were no doubt made and disseminated to other groups of grace believers. Apostolic letters were intended to be read aloud to the congregation much as they should be today. Picture the local believers gathering to hear Paul's letter read aloud. Ephesians 1:1-3:

1 Paul, an apostle of Jesus Christ by the

**will of God, to the saints which are at
Ephesus, and to the faithful in Christ Je-
sus: 2 Grace *be* to you, and peace, from
God our Father, and *from* the Lord Jesus
Christ.**

**3 Blessed *be* the God and Father of our
Lord Jesus Christ, who hath blessed us
with all spiritual blessings in heavenly
places in Christ:**

At the beginning of each of Paul's letters, we
will always find he includes these two words: *grace*
and *peace*. Since he is writing to believers familiar
with his gospel, he is affirming the *grace* of God
through His Son. No longer is the believer at enmity
with God. As such, they have *peace* with God and are
no longer subject to condemnation. During the Age
of Grace, the guilt of sin is not being held against sinners. Clemency is offered from God by *grace*. It is a
gift. For those who accept it, they now have *peace*
with God. In the future, sinners will once again be
subject to judgment, but not during this present age.
It is to those who have accepted this offer of salvation
by grace that Paul writes.

The next verse would seem to imply that God
has chosen those who are saved in advance. However, all verses must be interpreted within their con-

text. The verses end with two items. First, blessed is God. Second, God has blessed us *with all spiritual blessings in heavenly* places *in Christ.* Paul continues with this. Notice the action being done is by God the Father. Verse 4:

> **4 According as he [God] hath chosen us in him [Christ] before the foundation of the world, <u>that we should be holy and without blame before him in love:</u>**

Our state of *holiness,* meaning our separation from the world, and our blameless state have everything to do with our being *in Him* — our being *in Christ.*

We will see this as continuing theme in Ephesians. We, as grace believers, have been placed *in Christ.* It was this result which God predetermined in advance. It has nothing to do with predetermining the salvation of each individual. Verses 5-6:

> **5 [God] Having predestinated us unto the adoption of children by Jesus Christ to himself, according to the good pleasure of his will,**
>
> **6 To the praise of the glory of his [God's] grace, wherein he hath made us accepted <u>in the beloved</u>.**

This verse applies to those who, according to their free will, accept God's offer of salvation by grace. It is a gift for only those who accept it. To accept it, they must choose to believe it is true. It was predetermined, before the foundation of the world, that anyone who accepts God's offer of grace by faith would what? He predetermined that those who accept the offer will be accepted *in the Beloved – in Christ*. God determined that anyone who chose to believe the Gospel of Grace would be: (1) adopted by Jesus Christ and (2) made accepted *in the Beloved*. Friend, this is not about you and me. This is all about Christ and us being placed *in Him*.

Paul continues this theme of being *in Him* as he explains the riches of the gifts we will receive. These riches come from our position *in Him*. Verse 7:

> 7 **In whom [Christ] we have redemption through his blood, the forgiveness of sins, according to the riches of his [God's] grace;**

Note the reference to believers' position. They are *in Christ*. Again, it is this position to which all believers are predetermined by God. He determined in advance that anyone who chooses to believe His gracious offer of salvation will automatically be placed *in His Son*. Therefore, it is due to this position we

12

have redemption and forgiveness of our sins. We are redeemed! We were bought back by His blood. We are like slaves in the ancient marketplace. They had lost their freedom. As grace believers, we have been bought back from the slavery of sin, but there is more.

When we were bought back, we were then placed safely *in Christ*. We can be confident, as our eternal security is *in Him*. There are additional benefits because of our new position. Salvation is wonderful but there is so much more God has in store for them who love Him. What are these additional blessings? Verses 8-9:

> **8 Wherein [in which] he [God] hath abounded toward us in all wisdom and prudence; 9 Having made known unto us the mystery of his will, according to his good pleasure which he hath purposed in himself:**

Through Paul, God chose to reveal to us His eternal plan. The word *mystery* carries with it the connotation something was hidden. What is this mystery?

In his closing verses of his letter to the Romans, Paul refers to the revelation of the mystery as *my* gospel. God revealed this *mystery* to Paul which was once hidden but now is revealed. It is called the Gospel of Grace. Romans 16:25-26:

> **25 Now to him that is of power to [es]stablish you according to <u>my gospel</u>, and the preaching of Jesus Christ, <u>according to the revelation of the mystery</u>, which was kept secret since the world began,**

> **26 But now is made manifest [known], and by the scriptures of the prophets, according to the commandment of the everlasting God, <u>made known</u> to all nations for the obedience of faith:**

Let us look at the last verse in which God has now *made known to all nations for the obedience of faith.* Look at these two words *all nations.* Do you know who that is? The nations are the Gentiles. This mystery revealed to Paul is not being made known to the Gentiles. Finally, look at the words *for the obedience of faith. Faith* is *believing* what God said. *Obedience* is *complying with* or *accepting* the message that Paul is teaching! That is how Gentiles are saved.

It is God's desire to make Gentiles part of His redemption of Creation. This did not change any of His promises or prophecies to Israel. His ultimate plan is to make all subject to Christ. Now, stop for a moment and consider where grace believers are positionally. They are *in Christ,* right? Where is Christ's position now? He is seated at the right hand of God the Father in heaven. Ephesians 1:10:

> 10 **[So] That in the dispensation of the fulness of times he [God] might gather together in one all things <u>in Christ</u>, both which are in heaven, and which are on earth;** *even* **[that is to say] <u>in him</u>:**

Let us consider the words *in the dispensation of the fulness of times.* When something is full, you can no longer put anything more in. It is that concept that God is applying to the end times. During this period of time, when the ages are filled, God is sharing His plan with us. What is that plan? God's plan is for the overall Restoration of His Creation. The purpose is that *He might gather together in one all things in Christ.* All things would include everything in heaven and everything on earth — both Jews and Gentiles.

Paul now returns to writing about God's purpose for grace believers. Verse 11:

> 11 **In whom [Christ] also we have obtained an inheritance, being predestinated according to the purpose of him**

**who worketh all things after the coun-
sel of his own will:**

Paul, who was saved by grace, is writing to other grace believers in Ephesus. For that reason, he uses the word "we" when speaking about this inheritance. As part of God's purpose, He determined in advance to give those who, through faith believed, an inheritance. This *counsel of His Own will* includes God the Father, the Son, and the Holy Spirit.

It was through Christ's sacrifice that God could accomplish salvation for anyone who believes. Those who are saved by faith, God will bless them even more. The remainder of Ephesians will delve deeper into these blessings and protection. One might ask the question, "Why would God do this for us?" It is because we, with our free will, believed the good news of the Gospel of Grace. We trusted in God's Word. The moment we trusted His Word we were saved. When we were saved, God placed us in His Son. Where is His Son? He is seated beside God in heaven waiting for God to make His Son's enemies His footstool (*cf.* Ps. 110:1).

God knows those who believe are like rare gems. Those who have faith are like precious jewels because they trust His Word. God has consistently recognized acts of faith throughout the Bible. God gave Abraham the promise of becoming a great nation. We read about his response in Genesis 15:6:

6 And he believed in the LORD; and he counted it to him for righteousness.

God made a promise, Abraham believed His Word, and God accepted Abraham's faith as righteousness.

Faith is a requirement. We must believe in order to comply or be obedient to God's will. One must believe in order to accept God's offer of salvation by grace. Faith is not a work. Rather, it is mental assent or acknowledgement of the truth of God's Word. It was the same with Abraham. It was faith. It was his believing in God's Word that activated God's gift of righteousness. Prior to the point we believe them, they are just words.

Concerning that faith, Paul compares *faith* with *placing our trust in Christ.* Verse 12:

12 That we [who believe] should be to the praise of his glory, who first trusted in Christ.

Christ died for us. He did the work to purchase our redemption. There is nothing we can do but put our trust *in Him.* When we heard the gospel, we chose to believe. We trusted what God said is true. Paul refers to it as *the gospel of your salvation*. Hearing the gospel must precede believing. However, to hear it, someone must make the gospel, the good news, which was first made known to us. We must hear or read the words written by Paul. Either way, we must come to an understanding of the Gospel of Grace. We will come back to these words concerning those *who first trusted in Christ* in the next chapter.

If we understand it, then we can accept the offer. Verse 13:

> 13 **In whom [Christ] ye also *trusted*, after that ye heard the word of truth, the gospel of your salvation: in whom also after that ye believed, ye were sealed with that holy Spirit of promise,**

Once we hear and accept the offer by believing, then salvation is immediately received. God gives us the Holy Spirit. In the above verses, Paul refers to the Holy Spirit as *that holy Spirit of promise*. This is important for a reason.

A promise concerns something in the future. So, can a promise be something immediate or not? It can be now and in the future. In the same way a real estate transaction occurs, people make a promise. I have heard realtors say a home is sold once an offer is made and accepted. It is because of the promises that were made in the agreement to buy and sell the home. This is in spite of the fact that legally, according to the registry of deeds, the transaction has not yet been completed. Real estate transactions have two parts. There is the agreement and then there is the execution of that agreement. Paul explains the *holy Spirit of promise* in verse 14:

14 Which is the earnest of our inheritance until the redemption of the purchased possession, unto the praise of his glory.

Once His gracious offer of salvation has been accepted, the believer is immediately saved. Did you notice the word *earnest* in verse 14? This word has a legal meaning which comes from English Common Law. The word is still in use today in real estate transactions because it carries a specific meaning. *Earnest* is *a binding deposit or advance which serves to guarantee the fulfillment of a promise in the future.* You may ask, "Who is buying something?" The answer is, "God is!"

As grace believers, we are the purchased possession! We are the ones who Christ redeemed or bought back with His blood. He paid for us in full.

As a result of that transaction, we received the Holy Spirit when we believed. So, how is that holy Spirit of Promise acting as *earnest*? What is it that is not completed now but will be completed in the future? We will see in the next chapter.

3

Ephesians 1 (Part II)

At the time this epistle was written, news came by written letters or oral reports from eyewitness who traveled throughout the Roman Empire. Paul receives reports concerning various groups of grace believers he established. He had received favorable news concerning those in Ephesus. Verses 1:15-16:

> 15 **Wherefore I also, after I heard of your faith in the Lord Jesus, and love unto all the saints, 16 [I] Cease not to give thanks for you, making mention of you in my prayers;**

News of the Ephesian believers' faith had reached Paul and he was encouraged. He was constantly thanking God and praying for the grace believers. Since Ephesus was located on a major trade route connecting the Rome Empire, it provided ample opportunities for the Ephesians to show their hospitality and make the Gospel of Grace known. Let's go back and read Ephesians 1:12:

> 12 **That we should be to the praise of his glory, <u>who first trusted in Christ</u>.**

As grace believers, we should take every opportunity to share the Gospel of Grace with others. People cannot believe it unless they first hear the good news. Since we heard the gospel of our salvation first, before others, we should make it known. Once we have heard and understood the gospel of our salvation, Paul is saying that those who are the first to hear, are to bless others who have not. When we do this, we are to the praise of his glory!

Once we receive salvation by grace, there is no greater blessing than to gain a greater understanding of God's Word. That is what Paul prays. He desires that the Ephesians will continue to have their eyes opened to more knowledge of our Lord Jesus Christ. Ephesians 1:17:

> 17 **That the God of our Lord Jesus Christ, the Father of glory, may <u>give unto you the spirit of wisdom and revelation in the knowledge of him</u>:**

Paul asks God for two things on behalf of the Ephesians and, like them, us as well. He asks God to give (1) the spirit of wisdom and (2) the revelation of the knowledge of Him. Friend, there is no other way to obtain this than by reading the *Word of God*. The Spirit of Wisdom, of which Paul speaks, is the same Spirit Who inspired the writing of His Word. Now, we must depend upon this Spirit, which he calls the Spirit of Wisdom, to illuminate our understanding.

The Holy Spirit is the key to understanding the Bible. People who try to do it on their own find it confusing and often dry. However, one of our benefits God gives us is the Spirit of Wisdom. Why? It is through this Spirit of Wisdom that God can reveal Himself to us through His Word. There is a story about a pastor who said. "If you want to know what God is saying, then read the Bible. If want to hear God speak, then read the Bible out loud." The Bible is how God reveals Himself to us. It is the only way we gain wisdom and knowledge about Him.

Paul wants all believers, of which the Ephesians are representative, to grow in knowledge *of Him*. Paul takes us to an important reason wanting believers to have that knowledge. Paul is going to discuss the completion of the transaction. Do you remember to whom the *earnest* the holy Spirit of Promise was given? Now, read verse 18:

> 18 **The eyes of your understanding be-
> ing enlightened; that ye may know
> what is <u>the hope of his calling,</u> and what
> [is] <u>the riches of the glory of his inher-
> itance in the saints,</u>**

To this understanding, Paul adds the words *the hope of His Calling* and then something else. He adds words *the riches of the glory of his inheritance in the saints*. Wait a minute. An inheritance is something that is given to someone in the future. Paul is building this slowly so that we can understand it, yet I can hardly contain myself with excitement about what you are about to see.

Notice these words: *His inheritance.* It speaks about Christ's inheritance! His inheritance is *in the saints* – that is us! The saints or believers are Christ's inheritance! We were bought and paid for by His blood and God will give us to Christ. We are His and the glory of *His* inheritance!

In the following verses, this *exceeding greatness of His power* is directed towards us – those who believe. This power is compared to the same power of the resurrection which raised Christ from the dead. Verses 19-20:

19 And what *is* the exceeding greatness of his power to us-ward [toward us] who believe, according to <u>the working of his mighty power,</u>

20 <u>Which he wrought in Christ, when he raised him from the dead,</u> and set *him* at his own right hand in the heavenly *places*,

Note the position where Christ is located. After God raised Him from the dead, Christ was seated beside God in the heavens. We see a confirmation of this in Psalm 110:1:

1 The LORD said unto my Lord, Sit thou at my right hand, until I make thine enemies thy footstool.

David, King of Israel, wrote this psalm. In it, he refers to Elohim as LORD which is God, and Adonai as Lord which is Christ. The Lord Jesus Christ, Adonai, is seated at the right hand of God.

Paul continues by describing the preeminence and future position of the Risen Christ. And, as you read this, remember where grace believers are. They are all *in Christ.* Verses 21-23:

21 Far above all principality, and power, and might, and dominion, and every name that is named, not only in this world, but also in that which is to come:

22 And [God] hath put all *things* under his feet, and gave him *to be* the head over all *things* to the church, **23** Which is his body, the fulness of him that filleth all in all.

In the Restoration, we can see Christ will be placed far above all things. As grace believers, we are safe and secure *in Him*. The Lord Jesus Christ is the head and we are *the Body of Christ*.

4

Ephesians 2

It was Paul's prayer for grace believers to know the *hope of His Calling* and *the riches of the glory of his inheritance in the saints*. This is the goal he set for all grace believers. In the verses to follow, Paul will make these things known to us and, at the end, he will show us why they are so important.

Before we believed the gospel of our salvation, we were dead in our sins. We were not able to achieve salvation or make payment for our sins. Our good deeds do not negate our sins. If they did, there would be no reason that Christ should die for us. In view of our hopeless state, God provided the solution. When we heard the gospel of our salvation, we believed. When we believed, we were immediately saved and received the Holy Spirit as *earnest* to secure the fulfillment of *the promise*. Ephesians 2:1-2:

1 And you *hath he quickened* [made alive], who were dead in trespasses and sins;

2 Wherein in time past ye walked according to the course [ways] of this world, according to the prince of the power of the air, the [same] spirit that now worketh in <u>the children of disobedience</u>:

We were once dead in our trespasses and sins — for the wages or penalty of sin is death. Paul confirms this in his letters to the Roman believers and compares it to grace. Romans 6:23:

23 For the wages of sin is death; but the gift of God is eternal life through Jesus Christ our Lord.

Before our salvation, we operated according to the ways of the world — *the children of darkness* who have no light. We were under Satan's influence — the prince of the power of the air. We served the spirit of disobedience. We were rebellious and enemies of God.

Paul continues to describe our style or mode of living referring to it as *our conversation*. Verse 3:

3 Among whom also we all had our conversation in times past in the lusts of our flesh, fulfilling the desires of the flesh and of the mind; and were by nature the children of wrath, even as others.

In our fallen state, we served the flesh by seeking to fulfill our need for self-gratification. Despite this fallen state, God had mercy upon us. He showed His love towards us while we were still sinners. It was Christ Who made possible the reconciliation between sinners and their God. The following verses make this clear. Verses 4-5:

4 But God, who is rich in mercy, for his great love wherewith he loved us,

5 Even when we were dead in sins, hath quickened us [made us alive] together with Christ, (by grace ye are saved;)

Although we were dead in our sins, helpless, and at enmity with God, He quickened us or made us alive. Our salvation is instant. Why? Because God made those, who would be in Christ, alive at the same time He raised Christ from the dead. Can you see that? This was possible because of the power of the resurrection. Paul includes the parenthetical comment above to remind believers of an important fact. It is *by grace ye are saved!*

Once saved by grace through the power of the resurrection, grace believers are (1) sealed with the holy Spirit of Promise and (2) placed *in Christ.* Positionally, all grace believers are placed *in Him* spiritually. However, this does not mean that grace believers are physically *in Him.* Paul is going to deal with that subject shortly. Verses 6-7:

> 6 **And [God] hath raised *us* up together, and made *us* sit together in heavenly *places* <u>in Christ Jesus</u>:**

> 7 **That in the ages to come he might shew the exceeding riches of his grace in *his* kindness toward us <u>through Christ Jesus</u>.**

All the spiritual realm is watching this drama unfold. God is working towards His Restoration of Creation. These watchers and holy ones did not know God's plans for the Gentiles until He revealed this *mystery* to the Apostle Paul. They had no idea of the exceeding *riches of His grace* that God would show towards us *in Christ.*

The next two verses are two that are worthy of

memorization. If you write in your Bible, then please underline these verses! These are often quoted as they are the summary of Paul's Gospel of Grace. Verses 8-9:

> 8 For **by grace** are ye saved **through faith;** and that not of yourselves: *it is* the gift of God:
>
> 9 **Not of works,** lest any man should boast.

These words have specific meaning and, although, people can rattle the verses off, they often miss the central theological points. Grace is a *gift*. A *gift* is something given without expectation of repayment or creating an obligation of some form. In other words, *grace* is NOT *quid pro quo*. That is a Latin phrase that means *something for something*. To that end, we must realize that "giving our life to Christ" is not consistent with Paul's gospel. However, accepting His gracious offer is. Understanding the meaning of grace, in this context, is critical. As with any gift, it must be believed to be received. This gift of salvation is extended by the Giver to everyone, but it must be received, accepted, or believed, to be effective. It is our believing what God said that effects His gift of His Son's righteousness.

Although a gift is not paid for by the recipient, it came at a great cost to the Giver. It was paid for at the cost of His Beloved Son. Paul continues by making a very important point which is critical to the Gospel of Grace. There is nothing to be added! We can see that salvation is not by the works of man, but we must also see that works can add nothing. All the necessary work was completed at the Cross. Works would allow man to boast to both God and others that they had earned their salvation. Paul makes this clear in Romans 11:6:

> 6 **And if by grace, then is it no more of works: otherwise grace is no more grace. But if it be of works, then is it no more grace: otherwise work is no more work.**

This concept differentiates the Gospel of Grace from the Gospel of the Kingdom. We do not need to work for our salvation. We must receive it as a gift by believing God's Word. We cannot achieve our own righteousness. This would be contrary to Paul's gospel. Remember this: *Christ did it all!*

Having mentioned the concept of salvation not being from *works*, Paul goes on to elaborate. How do *works* come into play for those *saved by the grace of God?* Ephesians 2:10:

10 For <u>we are his workmanship</u>, created <u>in Christ Jesus</u> unto good works, which God hath before ordained that we should walk in them.

Let us take a moment and think about skilled *workmanship*. Like *craftsmanship*, it comes from the talent and skill that goes into making something worthy of admiration or notice. This would be like the skill of an architect or composer whose knowledge and expertise results in a finished masterpiece. Therefore, if we are the finished product of a master craftsman, who was this Craftsman. Certainly, it is not us. No, we were created by God and placed in Christ Jesus. The works that we do complete are those which He completes through us. We are His masterpiece. These are works that God *ordained* or *determined* we should do. If we have already received our salvation, then these works cannot be in payment of it. Rather, the works are the natural outflowing of being in *Christ Jesus*. We are *His* workmanship.

In the following verses, Paul speaks to the Gentiles. As was the custom at that time, righteous Jews who religiously followed the Law would have nothing to do with Gentiles. This was the case during Jesus' earthly ministry. Paul tells informs the Gentiles that Jesus came as the Messiah *in fulfillment of the promises God made to Israel*. Romans 15:8:

8 Now I say that Jesus Christ was <u>a minister of the circumcision</u> for the truth of God, <u>to confirm the promises made unto the fathers</u>:

The word *circumcision* refers to the Jews as it was the sign they followed the Abrahamic Covenant. The promises were made to Abraham, Isaac, and Jacob. They are the *fathers* to which Paul refers in this verse. He is speaking about the Gospel of the Kingdom which preceded Paul's receiving of the Gospel of the Grace. This gospel message will only be offered during this Age of Grace.

Jesus confirms Paul's statement above in the gospels. When Jesus sent out His twelve disciples, notice to whom this gospel message was sent. More specifically, to whom it was *not* directed. Matthew 10:5-6:

> **5** These twelve Jesus sent forth, and commanded them, saying, <u>Go not into the way of the Gentiles</u>, and into any city of the Samaritans enter ye not:
>
> **6** <u>But go rather to the lost sheep of the house of Israel</u>.

Now, with this information, let us continue

with verses Ephesians 2:11-12:

> **11 Wherefore remember, that ye** *being* **in time past Gentiles in the flesh, who are called Uncircumcision by that which is called the Circumcision in the flesh made by hands;**
>
> **12 That at that time ye were without Christ, being aliens from the common-wealth of Israel, and strangers from the covenants of promise, having no hope, and without God in the world:**

Notice the position of the Gentiles prior to God offering them salvation by grace through faith. They were aliens from the commonwealth of Israel, strangers from the covenants of promise, having no hope, and without God in the world! But now, this has all changed. How? It is because of what God has done for the Gentiles and anyone who chooses to accept His gift through His Son!

Paul begins with "but now" to make a comparison with today. Gentiles now have a way to receive salvation as a gift. Verses 13-14:

> **13 But now <u>in Christ Jesus</u> ye who sometimes were far off are made nigh by the**

blood of Christ.

14 For he is our peace, who hath made both one, and hath broken down the middle wall of partition *between us;*

Let's take a moment to discuss this *middle wall of partition.* During Paul's time, the Temple in Jerusalem was in full operation. There was a wall or division with warning signs posted. These were to prevent Gentiles, upon penalty of death, from entering the temple court which was reserved for the Jews only. It is this barrier to which Paul is referring as it separated the Jews from the Gentiles.

Christ has broken down what divided His creation: Jew and non-Jew. He brought these two divisions together thereby making peace between the two. How did Christ do this? Verse 15:

15 Having abolished in his flesh the enmity, *even* **[that is to say] the law of commandments** *contained* **in ordinances; for to make in himself of twain [the two] one new man,** *so* **[thereby] making peace;**

What was God's reason for doing this? It is His overall plan to reconcile the entire world to Himself through the Cross. Verses 16-18:

> **16 And that he might reconcile both [Jew and non-Jew] unto God in one body by the cross, having slain the enmity thereby:**
>
> **17 And came and preached peace to you which were afar off, and to them that were nigh. 18 For through him we both have access by one Spirit unto the Father.**

Through Christ, both Jews and Gentiles together, can have access to God through one Spirit. How does this union affect those now joined together? We will see they will both maintain their unique identity, but it is Christ Who is the singular source for both their salvations.

Speaking to the Gentiles, Paul draws a conclusion based on what he has presented thus far. Verse 19:

> **19 Now therefore ye are no more strangers and foreigners, but fellow-citizens with the saints, and of the household of God;**

He presents the overall picture of God's redemption of His Creation. This does not mean that the Jews and Gentiles are the same. Each one will continue to maintain their own identity. It is best explained this way. Creation is one, yet it is comprised of both heaven and earth. Together, these two make up God's singular Creation. Although they are one in view of Creation, heaven and earth still maintain their own unique characteristics.

Jews and Gentiles each receive revelation from God in different ways: apostles and prophets. Verse 20:

> 20 **And are built upon the foundation of the apostles and prophets, Jesus Christ himself being the chief corner** *stone;*

Paul ties everything together and places Jesus Christ at the center. It is Jesus Christ Who is the Chief Cornerstone. Let us look at another verse on this same subject. 1 Timothy 2:3-6:

> 3 **For this is good and acceptable in the sight of <u>God</u> our Saviour;** 4 <u>**Who will have all men to be saved, and to come unto the knowledge of the truth.**</u>
>
> 5 **For there is one God, and one mediator**

**between God and men, the man Christ
Jesus; 6 Who gave himself a ransom for
all, to be testified in due time.**

This foundation of which Paul writes in Ephesians is
the knowledge of the truth. He refers to foundational
doctrine or biblical teaching.

Concerning foundational doctrine, the knowledge of salvation comes from the teaching of God's
Word. Paul confirms this in Romans 10:14-15:

**14 How then shall they call on him in
whom they have not believed? and how
shall they believe in him of whom they
have not heard? and how shall they hear
without a preacher?**

**15 And how shall they preach, except
they be sent? as it is written, How beau-
tiful are the feet of them that preach the
gospel of peace, and bring glad tidings
of good things!**

First, we know it is God's will that all should come
to a saving knowledge. Second, we know we are
Christ's workmanship. Therefore, we should be ea-
ger to share with others the Gospel of Grace, right?
Once we are saved, then we are *in Christ* created *in*

Him to do good works. Third, we know our salvation is secure *in Christ.* Therefore, would it be consistent with God's will for us to share the message of salvation with others? Shouldn't this be first on our list of works which were ordained *in Him?*

Paul continues to focus on Jesus Christ Who is the *Chief Cornerstone.* Ephesians 2:21-22:

> 21 **In whom [Christ] all the building fitly framed together groweth unto an holy temple in the Lord: 22 In whom ye also are builded together for an habitation of God through the Spirit.**

These verses agree with Paul's writings to the grace believers in Colossae concerning the Body of Christ. Colossians 3:11:

> 11 **Where there is neither Greek nor Jew, circumcision nor uncircumcision, Barbarian, Scythian, bond nor free: but <u>Christ is all, and in all</u>.**

What a glorious thought! Christ is all in all!

5

Ephesians 3

Before we start this chapter, there are a few concepts with which you must be familiar. Shortly, you will see Paul writing about the *dispensation of the grace of God.* This word comes from a compound Greek word *oikonomia* from which we get our word *economy.* It is comprised of *oikos* which means *household* and *nomos* which means *law or ruling over.* So, *dispensation* would be a form of household stewardship. For our purposes, we will use the word *administration.* God has chosen to rule over His household or Creation using different administrations.

Although this book is not intended to teach about dispensations, it is important for you to be aware of them. The Bible can be divided into several dispensations which God uses to rule over or administrate His Creation. Here is a list of the first five of the dispensations which are generally accepted. Notice the parenthetical interruption called the Age of Grace. This Age of Law both precedes and follows the Age of Grace. At the end of the Age of Grace, the Age of Law will resume until Christ's Second Coming.

The First Five Dispensations

Name of Dispensation	Administrator
Innocence	Adam
Conscience	Noah
Nations or Human Government	
Promise	Abraham
Law	Moses
<< Age of Grace >>	<< Paul >>
Law — resumes	Moses

Today, churches are divided. Some choose to follow Moses and, fewer still, choose to follow Paul. Like a great highway that divides into two highways, we can only choose one. We cannot choose both. As you continue to study Paul's epistles, the choice becomes clear.

God chose Paul to be the Apostle to the Gentiles. When we first meet Paul, he is known as Saul and is present at and giving his approval of the stoning of Stephen. Paul was a pharisee and Stephen was the first martyr of the Kingdom Church. You can read the entire story in chapters 6 and 7 in the book of Acts. Saul later became Paul. We read in Acts 8:1:

> 1 **And Saul was consenting unto his [Stephen's] death. And at that time there was a great persecution against the church which was at Jerusalem; and they were all scattered abroad throughout the regions of Judaea and Samaria, except the apostles.**

Most Christians are familiar with the story of Paul's conversion on the Road to Damascus. Following his confrontation with the Risen Christ, Paul was blinded and taken by hand to Damascus. There, God spoke to a man named Ananias. He directed Anaias to go to Paul and lay his hands on him so that he might receive his sight. We find the dialogue between Anaias and God in Acts 9:10-18:

> 10 **And there was a certain disciple at Damascus, named Ananias; and to him said the Lord in a vision, Ananias. And he said, Behold, I am here, Lord. 11 And the Lord said unto him, Arise, and go into the street which is called Straight,**

and enquire in the house of Judas for one called Saul, of Tarsus: for, behold, he prayeth, 12 And hath seen in a vision a man named Ananias coming in, and putting his hand on him, that he might receive his sight.

13 Then Ananias answered, Lord, I have heard by many of this man, how much evil he hath done to thy saints at Jerusalem: 14 And here he hath authority from the chief priests to bind all that call on thy name. 15 <u>But the Lord said unto him, Go thy way: for he [Paul] is a chosen vessel unto me, to bear my name before the Gentiles, and kings, and the children of Israel: 16 For I will shew him how great things he must suffer for my name's sake.</u>

17 And Ananias went his way, and entered into the house; and putting his hands on him said, Brother Saul, the Lord, even [that is to say] Jesus, that appeared unto thee in the way as thou camest, hath sent me, that thou mightest receive thy sight, and be filled with the Holy Ghost. 18 And immediately there fell from his eyes as it had been scales:

and he received sight forthwith, and arose, and was baptized.

God told Ananias that He had chosen Paul to be His vessel or messenger. To whom was he to carry this important message?

God tells Ananias that Paul would "bear My name before the Gentiles, and kings, and the children of Israel" (v. 15). Remember, Paul is writing to the Gentiles in Ephesus during this current dispensation called the *Age of Grace*. With the above explanation, the meaning of the following verses should be clearer. Ephesians 3:1-2:

> 1 **For this cause I Paul, the prisoner of Jesus Christ for you Gentiles, 2 If ye have heard of <u>the dispensation of the grace of God which is given me</u> to you-ward:**

Paul was the first to be saved by grace and now is the Apostle to the Gentiles on behalf of Jesus Christ. He refers to himself as a prisoner since he is bound to his apostleship to deliver this unique gospel message to the Gentiles! Although directed to the Gentiles, it is available to any individual who believes, both Jew and Gentile.

From Whom did Paul receive this gospel message? It is clear in verses 3-4:

> 3 How that by revelation he [Christ] made known unto me the mystery; (as I wrote afore in few words, 4 Whereby, when ye read [this letter], ye may understand my knowledge in the mystery of Christ)

Most churches teach that Paul and the other Twelve Apostles carried the same message. They assume that, somehow, these apostles met up and exchanged notes to bring Paul up to speed. However., before the fateful confrontation on the Road to Damacus, Paul had never personally met the Lord Jesus Christ. Paul explains this to the Galatians. He writes in Galatians 1:15-19:

> 15 But when it pleased God, who separated me from my mother's womb, and called me by his grace, 16 To reveal his Son in [to] me, that I might preach him among the heathen [Gentiles]; immediately I conferred not with flesh and blood: 17 Neither went I up to Jerusalem to them which were apostles before me; but I went into Arabia, and returned again unto Damascus.

18 Then after three years I went up to Jerusalem to see Peter, and abode with him fifteen days. 19 But other of the apostles saw I none, save James the Lord's brother.

So, Paul remained separate from and did not meet any of the other apostles until three years in Arabia. He did not confer or consult with any other man which includes the other apostles. From these verses, we can glean it was Christ Himself Who taught the Apostle Paul for three years, then he returned to Damascus; not going to Jerusalem.

The good news which Paul received from the Risen Savior was given exclusively to him in the same way that the Law was given exclusively to Moses — face to face. Each was to distribute their respective messages to the intended recipients. Moses' Law went to the Jews. Paul's Grace went to the Gentiles. The content they received had not previously been given to anyone. Ephesians 3:5:

5 Which in other ages was not made known unto the sons of men, as it is now revealed unto his holy apostles and prophets by the Spirit;

The words *other ages* refer to past dispensations. During the current *Age of Grace,* the gospel message is called *The Gospel of the Grace of God.* You will see this confirmed in Paul's other epistles.

God would do something which He had kept as a secret or a *mystery.* It was not known by anyone. God would offer salvation to the Gentiles through the Apostle Paul. Verses 6-7:

> **6 That the Gentiles should be fellow-heirs, and of the same body, and partakers of his promise in Christ by the gospel:**

> **7 Whereof <u>I was made a minister,</u> according to <u>the gift of the grace of God</u> given unto me by the effectual working of his power.**

Paul was made the minister or *dispenser* of the gift of the grace of God during *the dispensation of Grace.* In the following verses, we see that Paul was given two tasks for his apostleship to the Gentiles. They are: (1) to preach the unsearchable riches of Christ and (2) to make known what is the fellowship of the *mystery.* We explained the reason it is called the *mystery* above. Verses 8-9:

> **8 Unto me, who am less than the least of**

all saints, is this grace given, that I should preach among the Gentiles the unsearchable riches of Christ;

9 And to make all *men* see what *is* the fellowship of the mystery, which from the beginning of the world hath been hid in God, who created all things by Jesus Christ:

In the spiritual realm, the watchers and the holy ones look on with great interest. They know Scripture well, but they had never seen or heard this before. With this new revelation to Paul, they could now see God's manifold wisdom — His ultimate purpose in His Son. Verses 10-11:

10 To the intent that now unto the principalities and powers in heavenly *places* might be known by the church the manifold wisdom of God, 11 According to the eternal purpose which he purposed in Christ Jesus our Lord:

Throughout his ministry, Paul suffered greatly for the privilege of bringing this news to the Gentiles and to the Jews who would listen as well. He preached and taught boldly because of the confidence he had *in Him*. Verses 12-13:

12 In whom we have boldness and access with confidence by the faith of him. 13 Wherefore I desire that ye faint not at my tribulations for you, which is your glory.

Paul receives his boldness and confidence from God. He constantly prayed for the needs of those to whom he ministered. They had received the message of grace and Paul wanted them to be strengthened in their faith. Like Paul, we need to be bold and confident enough in the gospel message to share it with others. Paul constantly prayed for this in the Ephesians as well as for all grace believers. In the following text, I added numbers in brackets to Paul's requests so that they stand out. Verses 14-19:

14 For this cause I bow my knees unto the Father of our Lord Jesus Christ, 15 Of whom the whole family in heaven and earth is named,

16 That he would grant you [grace believers], according to the riches of his glory, [1] to be strengthened with might by his Spirit in the inner man; 17 That [2] Christ may dwell in your hearts by faith; that [3] ye, being rooted and grounded in love, [4] 18 May be able to

comprehend with all saints what *is* the breadth, and length, and depth, and height; 19 And [5] to know the love of Christ, which passeth knowledge, that [6] ye might be filled with all the fulness of God.

Look at those six items again. The Apostle Paul knows the message of the Gospel of Grace better than anyone. The above list is what he earnestly prayed for the believers.

Paul remains consistent in this prayer for all the saints. Let us return to the beginning of his letter to see again what he wrote. Ephesians 1:16-19:

16 [I] Cease not to give thanks for you, making mention of you in my prayers;

17 That the God of our Lord Jesus Christ, the Father of glory, may give unto you the spirit of wisdom and revelation in the knowledge of him:

18 [That] The eyes of your understanding being enlightened; that ye may know what is the hope of his calling, and what the riches of the glory of his inheritance in the saints,

19 And to know the love of Christ, which passeth knowledge, <u>that ye might be filled with all the fulness of God.</u>

This letter was written to encourage the Ephesians and, for that matter, all grace believers to achieve this wisdom, knowledge, and understanding. We may ask, "To what end?" It is so we may know what is *the hope of His Calling* and what is *the riches of the glory of his inheritance in the saints.* Knowing this, we can understand the extent of Christ's love for us.

This amazing news had never been heard before the *mystery* was revealed to Paul. He finishes his thoughts and writes this wonderful doxology — words of praise to the One Who is the Giver of all our blessings *in Christ.* Verses 20-21:

20 Now unto him that is able to do exceedingly abundantly above all that we ask or think, according to the power that worketh in us,

21 Unto him *be* **glory in the church by Christ Jesus throughout all ages, world without end. Amen.**

6

Ephesians 4 (Part I)

Here is a question: Have you ever been so committed to a project or something you could not tear yourself away from it? It is almost as if you are compelled to continue or, perhaps, you feel bound to finish. It is the same with Paul towards his apostleship. For that reason, he refers to himself as a *prisoner of the Lord Jesus Christ.* He is impassioned or compelled to make known the good news about the Gospel of Grace. Between us, if Paul is a ten on a scale of one to ten, where are we for that same purpose? Due to this driven conviction, we can understand why he is brought to the point of imploring or pleading. Ephesians 4:1-3:

> 1 I [Paul,] therefore, the prisoner of the Lord, beseech you that ye walk worthy of the vocation wherewith ye are called,

2 With all lowliness and meekness, with longsuffering, forbearing one another in love; **3** Endeavouring to keep <u>the unity of the Spirit</u> in the bond of peace.

He writes similar instructions to the grace believers in Philippi. Philippians 2:2-4:

2 Fulfil ye my joy, that ye be like-minded, having the same love, being of one accord, of one mind.

3 Let nothing be done through strife or vainglory; but in lowliness of mind let each esteem other better than themselves. **4** Look not every man on his own things, but every man also on the things of others.

Haughtiness and self-centeredness have no place within the Body of Christ. Instead, each member should care for the well-being of the others. In his letter to the grace believers at Galatia, he lists the fruits of the Spirit. Galatians 5:22-23:

22 But the fruit of the Spirit is love, joy, peace, longsuffering, gentleness, goodness, faith, **23** Meekness, temperance: against such there is no law.

Above are the *characteristics* or lifestyle of grace believers who are *endeavoring to keep the unity of the Spirit in the bond of peace*. Returning to Ephesians, we see he continues with this concept of *unity*. Ephesians 4:4-7:

> 4 *There is* **one body, and one Spirit, even as ye are called in one hope of your calling;** 5 **One Lord, one faith, one baptism,**

> 6 **One God and Father of all, who** *is* **above all, and through all, and in you all.** 7 **But unto every one of us is given grace according to the measure of the gift of Christ.**

In the above verses, he uses the word "one" a total of eight times. Paul regularly uses repetition as a literary tool for teaching something important. Remember, his letters are written to be read aloud in the congregation.

Let's pause for a moment. How many churches can you think of that meet Paul's criteria? I cannot think of many. I must remember that the only person I have control over is me. Therefore, each of us can do our best to build *unity of the Spirit* with other grace believers. This is by no means works to earn salvation. We are his workmanship created in Jesus

Christ. Building unity in the Body of Christ are good works which were ordained in advance *in Christ.*

Paul chooses to use Psalm 68 as a reference because it expresses God's desire to bring all things under Himself through His Son. The beginning of the psalm gives us the context of being at the end times and the time of judgment. Psalm 68:1-3:

> 1 **Let God arise, let his enemies be scattered: let them also that hate him flee before him.**
>
> 2 **As smoke is driven away, so drive them away: as wax melteth before the fire, so let the wicked perish at the presence of God.**
>
> 3 **But let the righteous be glad; let them rejoice before God: yea, let them exceedingly rejoice.**

Now, we move to the closing verses of this Psalm. Verses 32-35:

> 32 **Sing unto God, ye kingdoms of the earth; O sing praises unto the Lord; Selah: 33 To him that rideth upon the heavens of heavens, which were of old; lo, he**

doth send out his voice, and that a mighty voice. 34 Ascribe ye strength unto God: his excellency is over Israel, and his strength is in the clouds.

35 O God, thou art terrible [frightful] out of thy holy places: the God of Israel is he that giveth strength and power unto his people. Blessed be God[!]

In view of the context of these final days of judgment, let us continue with Ephesians 4:8-10:

8 Wherefore he saith, When he [Christ] ascended up on high, he [Christ] led captivity captive, and gave gifts unto men.

9 (Now that he ascended, what is it but that he also descended first into the lower parts of the earth? 10 He that descended is the same also that ascended up far above all heavens, that he might fill all things.)

These verses end by restating God's ultimate plan. We have seen this before. This was the purpose that Christ must die according to the Scriptures! By doing this, He accomplished something incredible. Christ fulfilled the requirements of the Law!

It is interesting that Paul chose to use the word *captivity*. It may help to understand it as he uses this same word in another epistle. Romans 7:21-24:

> **21 I find then a law, that, when I would do good, evil is present with me. 22 For I delight in the law of God after the inward man:**
>
> **23 But I see another law in my members, warring against the law of my mind, and <u>bringing me into captivity to the law of sin</u> which is in my members. 24 O wretched man that I am! who shall deliver me from the body of this death?**

He is writing about the inability of the Law to make anyone righteous. As fallen people, we can try to attain righteousness on our own. However, we will continually fail and, in failing, we are condemned. Therefore, the *captivity* to which Paul refers is our *captivity* to sin. Paul shares his own struggles, calling himself wretched, in his deplorable and miserable state. He ends with this question: "Who shall deliver me from the body of this death?"

In Romans, he provides us with a detailed answer to this question. There is only one possible solution to this problem of sin. Romans 8:3-4:

> 3 **For what the law could not do, in that it was weak through the flesh, <u>God sending his own Son in the likeness of sinful flesh, and for sin, condemned sin in the flesh:</u>**

> 4 <u>**That the righteousness of the law might be fulfilled in us,**</u> **[in Christ], who walk not after the flesh, but after the Spirit.**

Friend, it is Christ's righteousness not ours that saves us! We who were not able, because of our *captivity to sin*, have been saved by Christ. He did all the work. Christ fulfilled the requirements of righteousness under the Law. Through our faith in His finished work, God imparts His righteousness to us—those who once had no hope.

In Romans 7, Paul speaks of a *dichotomy* which is *two warring parts of the whole*. Romans 7:25:

> 25 **I thank God through Jesus Christ our Lord. So then with the mind I myself serve the law of God; but with the flesh the law of sin.**

The Law of God for this current dispensation is grace with our righteousness paid for by Christ's blood. However, the Law of Sin convicts us in that we still sin in the flesh. Paul is speaking about the struggle grace believers will have while they tarry here on earth awaiting the *hope of His Calling* – the Rapture. God understands the power of sin for our human flesh. In Romans, Paul writes in Romans 5:20-21:

> 20 **Moreover the law entered, that the offence might abound. <u>But where sin abounded, grace did much more abound:</u>** 21 **That as sin hath reigned unto death, even <u>so might grace reign through righteousness unto eternal life by Jesus Christ our Lord</u>.**

There are many who will charge grace believers with teaching antinomianism which means "against the Law." This is not true. The Law still exists with its power to condemn. Christ solved this problem by fulfilling the Law. It is His righteousness, not ours, by which we are saved. He did not dismiss or revoke the Law. Christ fulfilled the Law!

Those who are saved by grace through faith are immediately saved and sealed with the holy Spirit of Promise. We discussed the meaning of the word *earnest* earlier. You may remember that the holy Spirit of Promise is the *earnest* which guarantees the fulfillment of the promise—our bodily redemption—at our calling. Now, in view of Paul's teaching on *capacity*, we see that, in our current state, our flesh still struggles under the weight of sin and condemnation under the Law. However, once the redemption of our body occurs, paid for by His blood and secured by the holy Spirit of Promise, the fulfillment of the purchase will be complete!

We know that, spiritually, we are *in Christ* Who is in the heavenlies. Our full redemption is secure *in Him.* It is guaranteed. We know that Christ is "far above all principality, and power, and might, and dominion, and every name that is named, not only in this world, but also in that which is to come" (Eph. 1:21). Right now, our bodies are here, and we struggle with sin in our members. God supports us while we wait for our bodily redemption. Ephesians 4:11-12:

> 11 **And he gave some, apostles; and some, prophets; and some, evangelists; and some, pastors and teachers; 12 <u>For the perfecting of the saints, for the work of the ministry, for the edifying of the body of Christ:</u>**

This earthly nurture and support will only be needed

temporarily. After the completion of our redemption, there will no longer be a need for it. Let's look at some verses about the Rapture.

To the grace believers in Thessalonica, Paul wrote to them telling them that, while waiting for this future event, they should comfort one another. 1 Thessalonians 4:15-18:

> 15 **For this we say unto you by the word of the Lord, that we which are alive and remain unto the coming of the Lord shall not prevent them which are asleep.**
>
> 16 <u>**For the Lord himself shall descend from heaven with a shout, with the voice of the archangel, and with the trump of God: and the dead in Christ shall rise first:**</u>
>
> 17 <u>**Then we which are alive and remain shall be caught up together with them in the clouds, to meet the Lord in the air: and so shall we ever be with the Lord.**</u> 18 **Wherefore comfort one another with these words.**

It is His appearing mid-air what marks what is referred to as *blessed hope – the hope of His Calling* (Eph. 1:18). We are to comfort and encourage one another with this wonderful hope. The Rapture is *the* completion of our full redemption. The word *Rapture* is Latin and comes from the Greek word *harpazo* which means *to snatch or catch away.* It refers to *His Calling* of His saints to Himself.

This is great news! The Rapture will happen *before* the Tribulation. This is called the *pre-tribulational* view and is supported by Scripture. The Tribulation is God's judgment upon the unrighteous. However, we are made righteous *in Christ.* Therefore, Paul writes to grace believers that they will be removed before the Tribulation. 1 Thessalonians 5:9-10:

> 9 **For God hath not appointed us to wrath, but to obtain salvation by our Lord Jesus Christ,** 10 **Who died for us, that, whether we wake [are still alive] or sleep [have passed away], we should live together with him.**

This, dear friend, is the fulfillment of our redemption which was guaranteed by the holy Spirit of Promise!

As we wait for our full redemption, what is it that Paul expects of us? Writing to Titus, he speaks about grace believers awaiting the *Blessed Hope.* Titus

2:11-14:

> 11 For the grace of God that bringeth salvation hath appeared to all men, 12 Teaching us that, denying ungodliness and worldly lusts, we should live soberly, righteously, and godly, in this present world;
>
> 13 <u>Looking for that blessed hope, and the glorious appearing of the great God and our Saviour Jesus Christ;</u> 14 Who gave himself for us, that he might redeem us from all iniquity, and purify unto himself a peculiar people, zealous of good works.

Let us return to Ephesians. Paul speaks about *the unity* of believers. It must be important since he repeats his desire for them. They are to come to the *knowledge of the Son of God* and *the stature of the fulness of Christ*. Ephesians 4:13:

> 13 Till we all come in the unity of the faith, and of the knowledge of the Son of God, unto a perfect man, unto the measure of the stature of the fulness of Christ:

Paul wants all grace believers, including the Ephesians, to grow in knowledge and, by so doing, to grow into *the stature of the fulness of Christ.* I think this is less about our own striving to be *in the likeness of Christ.* In my opinion, it is more about us being less self-driven and being more driven by Him. We need to be more dependent upon Him Who fills us—for Christ will be all in all.

This concept is somewhat repulsive to those who must do something in order to achieve something. Many Christians struggle with the concept that works do not play any part in our salvation. It is something that was offered to us as a gift, and we received it by accepting it. What if rather than struggling to be *a perfect man* and achieving *the measure of the stature of the fulness of Christ,* we stopped laboring in vain. Who are we to do this? Christ is *the head over all* things *to the church.* We are the church, *which is his body,* and *the fulness of Him that filleth all in all.*

The wisdom of Proverbs tells us, "For as he thinketh in his heart, so is he" (Prov. 23:7). It is the head that thinks. We are to take on the mind of Christ. Paul compares the natural man with the spiritual man in 1 Corinthians 2:14-16:

14 But the natural man receiveth not the things of the Spirit of God: for they are

foolishness unto him: neither can he know them, because they are spiritually discerned.

15 But he that is spiritual judgeth all things, yet he himself is judged of no man.

16 For who hath known the mind of the Lord, that he may instruct him? <u>But we have the mind of Christ</u>.

How is it that we can know the mind of Christ? Paul has been making that point all along. It is what he prayed for at the beginning of the letter. He prayed "that the Father of glory, may give unto you the spirit of wisdom and revelation in the knowledge of Him" (Eph. 1:17). What is the source of wisdom and revelation? It is the *Word of God*!

We will stop here so that you can think about this. Friend, we are at a critical point in Paul's teachings in Ephesians. When you are ready, we will continue with the remainder of Ephesians 4 in the next chapter.

7

Ephesians 4 (Part II)

So far, we know Christ completed all the work necessary for us to obtain our salvation. His death, burial, and resurrection established His righteousness that God offers to us as a gift — through grace by faith are we saved. We who believe are placed *in Christ* and our eternal salvation was secured *in Him*. We are redeemed spiritually, but our body or flesh remains here on earth. Paul teaches that grace believers, while waiting for their bodily redemption, must live worthy of *His Calling*. We ended the last chapter thinking about how that can be done.

Here are a few more verses to consider. Paul writes this to Timothy who was working with him. 2 Timothy 3:16:

16 **All scripture** is given by inspiration

of God, and is <u>profitable for doctrine,</u>
<u>for reproof, for correction, for instruc-</u>
<u>tion in righteousness:</u>

Paul follows this by stating its purpose. Verse 17:

17 **That the man of God <u>may be perfect,</u>**
<u>throughly</u> <u>furnished</u> <u>unto</u> <u>all</u> <u>good</u>
<u>works</u>.

Justification is the process by which God de-
clares that a sinner is righteous. Sanctification is the
process whereby God separates us from the worldly
things concerning your flesh. This applies also to His
work with the Jews. John 17:17:

17 **Sanctify them in the truth; your word**
is truth.

Thinking of this process of sanctifying the
Church — the Body of Christ, we will see this again in
Ephesians 5:25-27:

25 **. . . even as Christ also loved the**
church, and gave himself for it [the
Church]; 26 That he might sanctify and
cleanse it [His Body] <u>with the washing</u>
<u>of water by the word</u>, 27 That he might
present it [His Body] to himself a glori-

ous church, not having spot, or wrinkle, or any such thing; but that it should be holy and without blemish.

Reading and studying the *Word of God*, the Bible, sanctifies us. It separates us by the renewing of our mind. Our thoughts dwell on Christ Who is the *Word of God*. We have unity in the Church—Body of Christ—when all eyes are on the *Word of God*. Knowing this, Paul prays to *the Father of our Lord Jesus Christ* concerning all grace believers in Ephesians 3:18-19:

18 **[That they] May be able to comprehend with all saints what is the breadth, and length, and depth, and height;**

19 **And to know the love of Christ, which passeth knowledge, that ye might be filled with all the fulness of God.**

Paul's point is we must be filled with the knowledge and fulness of God. Is this to secure our salvation? No way! It is to secure both our minds, which is our thinking, and our hearts, which is our emotions. To do this, he is telling us that we must stay focused on God's Word. It must be ingrained in us! We are not alone. God not only provided us with His Holy Spirit and He also provided us with help during our earthly sojourn.

While we are here, God gave us apostles, prophets, evangelists, pastors, and teachers. They are to (1) perfect the saints for the work of the ministry and (2) to edify the body of Christ. Paul wants us to be mature believers. He does not want us to waver in our faith, but to reach *the measure of the stature of the fulness of Christ.* Ephesians 4:14:

> 14 **That we *henceforth* be no more children, tossed to and fro, and carried about with every wind of doctrine, by the sleight of men, *and* cunning craftiness, whereby they lie in wait to deceive;**

Hold fast the Word of Truth. In it, be firm and unwavering. This is the only way for us to act worthy of *His Calling.* When we do this, then we are one body, one Spirit, and one in the hope of *His Calling.* What is *His Calling?*

There are different meanings of the word *calling.* It is often used to refer to a ministry to which one is called. However, here, Paul is speaking of another *calling.* In his first letter to the Thessalonians, we will find the meaning. He precedes these verses with a discussion of the trials and tribulations which grace

70

believers are facing here. He assures them of the judgment of the evil ones who are the cause of this tribulation. Then, he writes of Christ's *calling* of His saints. This is referred to as the Rapture. 2 Thessalonians 1:10-12:

> 10 **When he shall come to be glorified in his saints, and to be admired in all them that believe (because our testimony among you was believed) in that day.**
>
> 11 **Wherefore also we pray always for you, <u>that our God would count you worthy of this calling</u>, and fulfil all the good pleasure of his goodness, and the work of faith with power:**
>
> 12 **That the name of our Lord Jesus Christ may be glorified in you, and ye in him, according to the grace of our God and the Lord Jesus Christ.**

The Rapture is only a partial fulfillment of God's plan of Restoration. There are three distinct groups of people on the earth. First there are the Gentiles, to which God called out Abraham to create a people separated to Himself. These are the Jews. Through the offer of salvation by grace through faith, God created a third group. The other group Paul refers to as neither Jew nor Gentile. That would be a third separate group. He mentions all three in one verse. 1 Corinthians 10:32:

> 32 **Give none offence, neither to [1] the Jews, nor to [2] the Gentiles, nor to [3] the church of God:**

The church is actually called the Body of Christ which He purchased with His blood. One out of three was saved by the Rapture. This leaves the remaining two groups to go through the testing of the Tribulation.

Let us return to our text where Paul focuses on the interaction between grace believers awaiting the *Blessed Hope*. Ephesians 4:15-16:

> 15 **But speaking the truth in love, may grow up [mature] into him in all things, which is the head,** *even* **[which is to say] Christ:**
>
> 16 **From whom the whole body fitly joined together and compacted by that which every joint supplieth, according to the effectual working in the measure of every part, maketh increase [growth] of the body unto the edifying of itself in**

love.

Each believer is a member of the Body of Christ of which Christ Himself is the Head. At *His Calling,* these members of the Body of Christ will be fitted together as one. This is the unity of which he wrote previously. Now, he writes of both our future state as well as our earthly state. Any individual cares for their body. So too, the Body of Christ is to care for itself in love.

Paul now turns his attention to what he calls *our conversation.* He means our current *lifestyle* or *mode of living.* He is concerned about our human nature. It is in our fallen natures to act in self-interest and look after our own personal advancement or benefit. He gives us examples of self-centeredness in verses 17-19:

> 17 **This I say therefore, and testify in the Lord, that ye henceforth walk not as other Gentiles walk, in the vanity of their [own] mind,**
>
> 18 **Having the [their] understanding darkened, being alienated from the life of God through the ignorance that is in them, because of the blindness of their heart:**

19 Who being past [beyond] feeling have given themselves over unto lasciviousness, to work all uncleanness with greediness.

He knows the wickedness of the flesh and the natural desires of the heart. These are damaging both to the individual as well as to the Body of Christ in general.

These are not the character of Christ. We are to put off our former *conversation*. We are to change our lifestyle, our mode of living. We are to put off our former lifestyle. Verses 20-22:

20 But ye have not so learned [these things from] Christ; 21 If so be that ye have heard him, and have been taught by him, as the truth is in Jesus:

22 <u>That ye put off concerning the former conversation the old man</u>, which is corrupt according to the deceitful lusts;

In a similar manner, he teaches the grace believers in Corinth that we are now new creatures *in Christ*. 2 Corinthians 5:17:

17 Therefore if any man be in Christ, he is a new creature: old things are passed

away; behold, all things are become new.

As our spirits have been renewed, so should our minds be renewed. By so doing, we become a new man in the likeness of Christ Who is both righteous and holy. Ephesians 4:23-24:

> 23 **And be renewed in the spirit of your mind; 24 And that ye put on the new man, which after God is created in righteousness and true holiness.**

How is this done? Paul provides us with a list of actions we must take to accomplish this. Verses 25-29:

> 25 **Wherefore putting away lying, speak every man truth with his neighbour: for we are members one of another.**

> 26 **[If] Be ye angry, and [then] sin not: let not the sun go down upon your wrath: 27 Neither give place to the devil.**

> 28 **Let him that stole steal no more: but rather let him labour, working with** *his* **hands [doing] the thing which is good, that he may have to give to him that needeth.**

29 Let no corrupt communication proceed out of your mouth, but that which is good to the use [purpose] of edifying, that it may minister grace unto the hearers.

Reading this, we see that it can be summed up in this way. We are to treat others, especially other grace believers, in love and doing to them as we would have done to us. We should treat others knowing how Christ first loved us while we were still sinners.

The next verse refers to the holy Spirit of Promise. It was by Him that we were sealed for the promised redemption — *His calling unto Himself*. We are not to grieve or sadden Him by our actions. Verse 30:

30 And grieve not the holy Spirit of God, whereby ye are <u>sealed unto the day of redemption.</u>

Now, Paul turns to believers' interactions with people in general. Verse 31:

31 Let all bitterness, and wrath, and anger, and clamour, and evil speaking, be put away from you, [along] with all malice:

He concludes by directing his remarks to the fellowship of believers saved by grace through faith. It is Paul's desire for grace believers to thrive and grow in the faith. Therefore, the health and unity of the Body of Christ is dependent upon the care shown by its individual members. Verse 32:

> 32 And be ye kind one to another, tenderhearted, forgiving one another, even as God for Christ's sake hath forgiven you.

8

Ephesians 5

Paul loves the grace believers like they were his own children. In his first letter to Timothy, he writes to him as "my own son in the faith" (1 Tim. 1:2). In this chapter, he continues to provide grace believers with guidance on how they should live in a way that is acceptable to God. Again, while spiritually in Christ, the body remains in this fallen world.

He points out that we are children of God through His Son and, for that reason, we should act accordingly. Like a royal family who is always in the spotlight, we too are expected to act in a manner representative of our King. We are to love other believers as members of the King's family. Ephesians 5:1-2:

> **1 Be ye therefore followers of God, as dear children; 2 And walk in love, as**

Christ also hath loved us, and hath given himself for us an offering and a sacrifice to God for a sweet-smelling savour.

Many of the sacrifices offered under Old Testament Law were considered by God to have a pleasing aroma. Think for a moment about the holidays when the turkey or roast was cooking. The smell filled the home. Many of us found that pleasing.

As His children, we are to refrain from certain activities. Not only are they contrary to the *Word of God*, but they are dangerous to both our physical health and spiritual well-being. Verses 3-5:

> 3 **But fornication, and all uncleanness, or covetousness, let it not be once named among you, as becometh saints;**
>
> 4 **Neither filthiness, nor foolish talking, nor jesting, which are not convenient [suitable]: but rather giving of thanks.**
>
> 5 **For this ye know, that no whoremonger [one who seeks out prostitutes], nor unclean person, nor covetous man, who is an idolater, hath any inheritance in the kingdom of Christ and of God.**

Paul discusses grace believers' relationships with non-believers. Children of disobedience are those who are contrary to God. They are children of darkness. They serve and are controlled by the god of this world. Verse 6-7:

> 6 **Let no man deceive you with vain words: for because of these things cometh the wrath of God upon the children of disobedience. 7 Be not ye therefore partakers with them.**

We were once children of disobedience. But now, we are children of light—those saved by grace. He charges us to act accordingly since we know that all grace believers are *in Christ.* Verses 8-10:

> 8 **For ye were sometimes darkness, but now** *are ye* **light <u>in the Lord</u>: <u>walk as children of light</u>:**
>
> 9 **(For the fruit of the Spirit** *is* **in all goodness and righteousness and truth;)**
>
> 10 **Proving what is acceptable unto the Lord.**

By separating ourselves from darkness, we renew our minds and walk *in Christ.* Paul provides a list to be *holy* which means to be separated to God. Verses 11-13:

> 11 And have no fellowship with the un-fruitful works of darkness, but rather reprove [admonish or correct] *them.*

> 12 For it is a shame even to speak of those things which are done of [by] them in secret.

> 13 But all things that are reproved are made manifest [made know] by the light: for whatsoever doth make manifest is light.

Speaking about believers who are not paying attention or acting inappropriately, he refers to them as sleeping. My grandfather used to say that some-one needed to snap their suspenders. Perhaps, this is more of an opened-hand-tap to the back of the head. Awake up! Christ is the light. Verses 14-18:

> 14 Wherefore he saith, Awake thou that sleepest, and arise from the dead, and Christ shall give thee light. 15 See then that ye walk circumspectly [prudently or carefully], not as fools, but as wise,

16 Redeeming [making use of] the time, because the days are evil. **17** Wherefore be ye not unwise, but understanding what the will of the Lord is.

18 And be not drunk with wine, wherein is excess; but be filled with the Spirit;

We are told not to be unwise, but instead to understand the will of the Lord. One may ask, "How shall we be wise?" or "What is the source of wisdom?" It is the *Word of God*. The Bible is our singular source of wisdom and understanding the will of the Lord!

Paul has consistently maintained the same message. From his prayer at the beginning of Ephesians where we read this in Ephesians 1:17-18:

17 That the God of our Lord Jesus Christ, the Father of glory, may give unto you <u>the spirit of wisdom and revelation in the knowledge of him:</u>

18 The eyes of <u>your understanding being enlightened;</u> that ye may <u>know what is the hope of his calling, and what the riches of the glory of his inheritance</u> in the saints,

Think of how much we have learned so far from this short letter to the Ephesians. We must continue to study, as we are now, the *Word of God*. Paul instructed Timothy, his son in the faith, to "study to shew thyself approved unto God, a workman that needeth not to be ashamed, rightly dividing the word of truth" (2 Tim. 2:15).

Being filled with the Spirit we are to have joy in this life as we await our bodily redemption, also known as the Rapture. Wait, did I just say *joy?* These are his suggestions to live a *joyous* life. Verses 19-21:

> 19 **Speaking to yourselves [one another] in psalms and hymns and spiritual songs, singing and making melody in your heart to the Lord;**
>
> 20 **Giving thanks always for all things unto God and the Father in the name of our Lord Jesus Christ; 21 Submitting yourselves one to another in the fear of [respect for] God.**

This is how we, as grace believers, should act towards each other: rejoice together, give thanks together, and be humble out of our respect for God.

Paul moves onto a different relationship. The

importance of marriage in God's Creation was laid out at the beginning with Adam and Eve. He now writes about marriage and this special relationship beginning with the wives. Verses 22-24:

> 22 **Wives, submit yourselves unto [respect] your own husbands, as unto the Lord.**
>
> 23 **For the husband is the head of the wife, even [that is to say] as Christ is the head of the church: and he is the saviour of the body.**
>
> 24 **Therefore as the church is subject unto Christ, so** *let* **the wives** *be* **[subject] to their own husbands in every thing.**

Then, he continues with the husbands. Verses 25-30:

> 25 **Husbands, love your wives, even as Christ also loved the church, and gave himself for it;** 26 **That he might sanctify and cleanse it with the washing of water by the word,** 27 **That he might present it to himself a glorious church, not having spot, or wrinkle, or any such thing; but that it should be holy and without blemish.**

28 So ought [should] men to love their wives as their own bodies. He that loveth his wife loveth himself. 29 For no man ever yet hated his own flesh; but nourisheth and cherisheth it, even [that is to say] as the Lord [does] the church: 30 For we are [all] members of his body, of his flesh, and of his bones.

Paul concludes with the most important relationship of all — the one upon which civilization itself was built. He addresses the foundation of the family — the relationship between a husband and a wife. He explains the mystery of this relationship by comparing it with Christ and His Church being like the union between a man and a woman. Verses 31-33:

31 For this cause shall a man leave his father and mother, and shall be joined unto his wife, and they two shall be one flesh. 32 This is a great mystery: but I speak concerning Christ and the church.

33 Nevertheless let every one of you in particular so love his wife even as himself; and the wife *see* that she reverence [respect] *her* husband.

Paul, inspired by God, is speaking about the God-ordained union between a husband and a wife. This relationship is so unique that he compares it to the relationship between Christ and His church.

9

Ephesians 6 (Part I)

Paul continues to present what is a good and acceptable way for grace believers to act before the Lord. Grace believers are the *children of light* and are held to a higher standard than the *children of darkness.* Having just dealt with the foundational relationship between a husband and a wife, he turns his attention to the family. Ephesians 6:1-3:

> 1 **Children, obey your parents in the Lord: for this is right. 2 Honour thy father and mother; (which is the first commandment with promise;) 3 That it may be well with thee, and thou mayest live long on the earth.**

Of the ten commandments given to Moses, the one commanding children to obey their parents came with a blessing. Let's look at Exodus 20:12:

12 Honour thy father and thy mother: that thy days may be long upon the land which the LORD thy God giveth thee.

Fathers are to provide structure and discipline. Here, the word *discipline* means *teaching*. Paul uses the word *nurture* could be compared to the way a gardener *cares for and oversees his garden*. He sees the children get what they need to grow up healthy and bear fruit. While the word *admonish* is more directional. It means *to guide, correct, advise, teach, and warn*. Ephesians 6:4:

4 And, ye fathers, provoke not your children to wrath: but bring them up in the nurture and admonition of the Lord.

It is important for a father maintains a balance and not become overbearing. Correction can make a child frustrated but, to do it excessively, creates an angry child. Think about an ax on a grinding wheel. The right amount of pressure sharpens the tool. Grinding it too hard, leaves you with nothing but the handle.

The role of the servant during biblical times can be compared with today's employee. Paul addresses employees first. Verses 5-8:

5 Servants, be obedient to them that are *your* masters according to the flesh, with fear and trembling, in singleness of your heart, as unto Christ;

6 Not with eyeservice, as men-pleasers; but as the servants of Christ, doing the will of God from the heart;

7 With good will doing service, as to the Lord, and not to men: 8 Knowing that whatsoever good thing any man doeth, the same shall he receive of the Lord, whether *he be* bond or free.

He turns his attention to employers referring to them as *masters.* Verse 9:

9 And, ye masters, do the same things unto them, forbearing threatening: knowing that your Master also is in heaven; neither is there respect of persons with him.

In what is called *free will* employment, there are no slaves or indentured servants. They are free to leave whenever they wish and, while they are at work, there are certain legal protections. It comes down to this as a guiding light. Whether an employer or employee, as grace believers, we must act in a way that is glorifying to God, our Savior.

Let us stop for a moment and summarize some facts we know. We are saved by what God did for us through His Son and there is nothing we can add to either earn or maintain our salvation. It is a gift we receive through faith. Faith is believing. It is our mental assent that the *Word of God* is true concerning Christ's death, burial, and resurrection as it applies to our salvation. We trusted in it and, the moment we did, we were saved.

As a guarantee, we received the holy Spirit of Promise Who is placed in us. He resides in us. We are then immediately placed *in Christ.* He bought us with His blood. We are redeemed, or bought back from our fallen state, and we are placed *in Him.* It is important we know this as it pertains to our eternal security. Paul states this clearly in his letter to the Romans. Notice the interchangeability of the words *through Him that loved us* with the words *in Him.* Romans 8:37-39

> 37 **Nay, in all these things we are more than conquerors <u>through him that loved us.</u>**
>
> 38 **For I am persuaded, that neither**

death, nor life, nor angels, nor principalities, nor powers, nor things present, nor things to come,

39 Nor height, nor depth, nor any other creature, shall be able to separate us from the love of God, which is in Christ Jesus our Lord.

Should you ever be challenged with a question like, "How secure are you in the love of God?" Your answer should be nothing short of, "Very secure!" As grace believers, we *have been* redeemed. We *have been* bought back and are presently secure *in Christ*.

Although we are spiritually placed *in Christ,* we must remain on this earth in our present bodies — our flesh. We must remain here until *our calling* which is the Rapture. There is an important reason we remain here. God entrusted all grace believers a purpose. In his second letter to the Corinthians, Paul describes our mission. 2 Corinthians 5:17-18:

17 Therefore if any man be in Christ, he is a new creature: old things are passed away; behold, all things are become new. 18 And all things are of God, who hath reconciled us to himself by Jesus Christ, and hath given to us the minis-

<u>try of reconciliation;</u>

Some may argue that this ministry was given to Paul and his associates alone, but I would disagree. It was given to every grace believer. He continues with the words *to wit* which means *namely* or *that is to say.* Verses 19-21:

> 19 **To wit, that God was in Christ, reconciling the world unto himself, not imputing their trespasses unto them; and <u>hath committed unto us the word of reconciliation.</u>**

> 20 **Now then <u>we are ambassadors for Christ</u>, as though God did beseech you by us: we pray you in Christ's stead, be ye reconciled to God.**

> 21 **For he [God] hath made him [Christ} to be sin for us, who knew no sin; <u>that we might be made the righteousness of God in him</u> [in Christ].**

We remain here, bodily, we are to make known the mystery of the Gospel of Grace. This is consistent with God's will. What is that will? Paul writes of this in his letter to Timothy who had himself become a minister of reconciliation with the Gospel of Grace.

1 Timothy 2:3-4:

> **3 For this is good and acceptable in the sight of God our Saviour; 4 Who will have all men to be saved, and to come unto the knowledge of the truth.**

It was Paul's desire for the Ephesians to grow and mature in the faith. He wants each believer to fully come to the knowledge of this truth so that they will share what they know with others.

Of these grace believers who are saved and filled with wisdom and revelation in the knowledge of him, we could say they are "armed and dangerous." You could ask, "Dangerous to whom?" The opposition is always watching As ambassadors of reconciliation, we must "make known the mystery of the gospel" (Eph. 6:19). During our sojourn here on earth, did God leave us in these frail bodies defenseless against this adversary. In the next chapter, we will continue with Ephesians 6 where Paul teaches on our defense against the assaults of the adversary.

10

Ephesians 6 (Part II)

We are creatures with a mind as well as emotions or feelings. This is how God created us. God is always our Provider, Protector, and Great Savior. While we are here, He is with us. His holy Spirit of Promise secures us. Having us remain here in our body until *our calling* is not an accident. It is part of His plan. In addition to the Holy Spirit which resides within us, God has also provided us with a means by which we can protect and defend ourselves.

In the remainder of this chapter, Paul writes to every grace believer. I love the great doctrinal hymns. The words from *A Mighty Fortress Is Our God* are very apropos for us here.

A mighty fortress is our God
A bulwark never failing

Our helper He amid the flood
Of mortal ills prevailing
For still our ancient foe
Doth seek to work us woe
His craft and pow'r are great
And armed with cruel hate
On earth is not his equal

The adversary is fierce and wily. He can steal our *joy*, but he can never defeat us! Paul speaks like a coach in the locker room before a major game. He offers us last-minute encouragement and instruction. How are we to defend ourselves against the adversary? Ephesians 6:10-11:

> 10 **Finally, my brethren, be strong in the Lord, and in the power of his might.**
> 11 **Put on the whole armour of God, that ye may be able to stand against the wiles of the devil.**

Paul goes into detail explaining this armor of God which is our defense. This is figurative but a means by which we can remember each piece and its purpose. Try to see yourself putting on each piece.

He tells us who the enemies are. Satan is a wily or crafty adversary in constant pursuit of all he may devour — specifically those who are unsaved. When

Lucifer rebelled against God, he took with him one-third of the angels. In a moment, you will see these rebels referred to as *principalities, powers,* and *the rulers of the darkness of this world.* Satan has lost those saved by grace but be believes the unsaved belong to him. They are the *children of darkness.* Satan will fight to subvert any attempt to rescue the lost—what he believe is his possession. He does this by slowing or stopping the advance of the gospel message. Satan is not working alone. Paul speaks of another dimension called the spiritual realm of which some may be aware. Verse 12:

12 For we wrestle not against flesh and blood, but against principalities, against powers, against the rulers of the darkness of this world, against spiritual wickedness in high *places.*

There is a hierarchy within this spiritual realm with Satan as its head.

We find an excellent example of this in the book of Daniel. Daniel was a prophet and prayed to God on behalf of Israel, like Paul, making requests. His prayer was heard, and God sent a response. However, the *angel* acting as God's *messenger* was delayed. We learn of a spiritual battle in which this angel was a participant. In the following verses, the Angel Gabriel explains the delay. Daniel 10:12-13:

> **12 Then said he unto me, Fear not, Daniel: for from the first day that thou didst set thine heart to understand, and to chasten thyself before thy God, thy words were heard, and I am come for thy words. 13 But the prince of the kingdom of Persia withstood me one and twenty days: but, lo, Michael, one of the chief princes, came to help me; and I remained there with the kings of Persia.**

Michael and Gabriel are both angels and servants of God. Their counterparts serve Satan. These are the same ones with which we *battle against principalities, powers, rulers of the darkness of this world, and spiritual wickedness in high* places.

Paul wants us to be prepared to defend ourselves against these adversaries. Notice the armor of God is defensive! The final battle will be won when the King returns to claim Israel at the Battle of Armageddon. We are to stand; not to fight! Ephesians 6:13:

> **13 Wherefore take unto you the whole armour of God, that <u>ye may be able to withstand in the evil day, and having done all, to stand.</u>**

You will see, in a moment, that the battles belong to the Lord, the *Word of God*. The word *withstand* means to *remain standing* and not to fall. Notice the words with which he begins the next verse, *Stand therefore!* We are not to shrink or run away, but instead *Stand!* Verse 14:

> 14 Stand therefore, **having your loins girt about with truth, and having on the breastplate of righteousness;**

Our loins are where our two legs come together. Picture yourself placing both of your feet firmly and standing so that you cannot be knocked down. What are you standing on? Look back to the prayer with which Paul opened this letter. Ephesians 1:17:

> 17 **That the God of our Lord Jesus Christ, the Father of glory, may give unto you the spirit of wisdom and revelation in the knowledge of him:**

This is the central theme of Ephesians: understanding and knowing God and all that concerns us as grace believers. We must know God's Word. We must firmly stand on that knowledge. Can you see how important the *Word of God* is and how important we know it?

Think about your confidence in your position *in Christ*. Do you have any doubt about His love for you? Do you have any doubt of your salvation according to His promises? If you have no doubt, then you can plant both your feet firmly on the truth! If our beliefs are ever challenged, our ability to stand firmly on these promises of God will keep us from being knocked down. With our loins firmly girded, or tightly wrapped, with the truth, it provides us with the ability to stand firmly. What are we standing upon? We stand upon the *Word of God!* We are *Standing on the Promises!*

You saw his reference to *the breastplate of righteousness*. The breastplate is the armor that protects the heart—our emotions. Friend, each of us is human and we all have emotions including fear. When we think about righteousness, is it not our righteousness which will uphold us. No, it is Christ's righteousness. We have the righteousness of Christ because God imparted it to us. When we think of the heart, we think about our emotions. There is nothing that can separate us from the love of God. *Nothing!* Therefore, the breastplate of righteousness *is Christ!* Remember this in the battle. Regardless of what ever words someone hurls against us, we have Christ's righteousness. Nothing can shake our confidence in this because we are *in Christ!*

We continue with Ephesians 6:15:

15 And your feet shod with the prepara-tion of <u>the gospel of peace</u>;

Paul uses a reference to feet concerning *the gospel of peace* in Romans 10:14-15:

14 How then shall they call on him in whom they have not believed? and how shall they believe in him of whom they have not heard? and how shall they hear without a preacher?

15 And how shall they preach, except they be sent? as it is written, <u>How beau-tiful are the feet of them that preach the gospel of peace, and bring glad tidings of good things!</u>

These feet represent someone who carries the good news. They bring the gospel of salvation. Doing this, we fulfill the will of God that all should come to a saving knowledge of the truth. When our love for God overflows, we share the good news with others!

The shield is another defensive part of armor. Its intent is to protect against an assault or barrage of an incoming attack of arrows. During Roman times, these arrows would be dipped in something flammable and shot at their enemies. Verse 16:

16 Above all, taking the <u>shield of faith</u>, wherewith ye shall be able to quench all the fiery darts of the wicked.

It is my belief that these are personal attacks on both the individual believer as well as groups. I have been asked whether these attacks could be made on our health and personal property. The text does not specifically mention how these attacks may be made. If it affects our faith or relationship with God, then it may be possible. Remember, we are His. We were bought and paid for with a price.

Believers are members of the family of God through Christ. The extent of Satan's powers is limited by our Sovereign God. As with Job, we have a hedge of protection around us. When Satan was testing Job, he realized his scope was limited by God. Satan argues with God in Job 1:10-12:

10 Hast not thou made an hedge about him, and about his house, and about all that he hath on every side? thou hast blessed the work of his hands, and his substance is increased in the land.

11 But put forth thine hand now, and touch all that he hath, and he will curse thee to thy face.

12 And the LORD said unto Satan, Behold, all that he hath is in thy power; only upon himself put not forth thine hand. So Satan went forth from the presence of the LORD.

We cannot know the ways of God for they are higher than ours. We are to hold firmly to our faith. When we continue to trust Him, we are putting that faith into action!

The next two items on Paul's list are the helmet and the sword. We will handle each separately as they have different purposes in our defense. Verse 17:

17 And take the helmet of salvation, and the sword of the Spirit, which is the word of God:

The purpose of the helmet is to protect the head. It refers to our mind where we think. It is the center of rational thought which makes mankind unique from all other creatures. Since our thoughts are not impervious to outside influence, the head needs protection. This helmet is special. Paul refers to it as *the helmet of salvation.*

We must keep the Source of our salvation in the forefront of our mind. Everything we do, see, or think must be done within the perspective of our eternal salvation. An example will best serve our purpose. Let's say you lose your job, receive an eviction notice, your car is hit by another car, and you have a fight with your best friend. Let's say this all happens the same day. What would you be thinking? The helmet is to protect your head — your mind. You have doubts about God's love and His plans for you. This is an example of how Satan attacks us.

When something like this happens, first, we should start by reciting the truths you know. If possible, try to see the situation in the grand scope of eternity. See these events through the eyes of faith. We are still saved. Our salvation is secure. We are members of God's family. We can boldly walk into His presence at any time. Then, having the full knowledge of God's Word, you remember Paul's letter to the grace believers in Philippians 4:6-7:

> 6 **Be careful [anxious] for nothing; but in every thing by prayer and supplication with thanksgiving let your requests be made known unto God.**

7 And the peace of God, which passeth all understanding, shall keep your hearts and minds through Christ Jesus.

The word *careful* literally means *full of care*. So, do not be anxious or full of care *for anything!* This is followed by the word "but" then Paul proceeds to list what we should do. You were just about to reach for the ejector lever. When your thinking returns, you start to recall all of those promises in God's Word!

The first rule in any emergency is: Remain calm! Stand firm! Do not allow yourself to be knocked over. Prayer is talking to God. So, pick up your spiritual phone and talk to Him. You can handle that. Make your supplications or requests known to Him. Tell Him your problems or issues (as if He didn't ready know). Then, ask Him for help. Try to mingle your requests with thanksgiving even if you must struggle to find something for which you can be thankful. Believe it or not, the process of giving thanks is to benefit you! It reassures you of your blessings and your position with God! It is your mind which must be protected. Your knowledge of God and your eternal security in Him are your helmet of salvation. Any event or disaster cannot change your position or relationship with God. Of this, you can be confident!

I am sure you have noticed a central theme from the beginning and throughout this letter. Ephesians 1:17:

> 17 **That the God of our Lord Jesus Christ, the Father of glory, may give unto you <u>the spirit of wisdom and revelation in the knowledge of him</u>:**

We will finish our study of Ephesians 6 in the next chapter.

11

Ephesians 6 (Part III)

We are almost finished with Paul's armor of God. This is the grace believer's primary defense until *His Calling*. The last item is *the sword of the Spirit*. The sword is the most powerful of our defenses. Roman centurions considered their sword and their shield to be the most valuable parts of their armor. The author of Hebrews writes to the kingdom believers, but his writings being part of Scripture, provide an excellent reference for *the sword of the Spirit*. Hebrews 4:12:

> 12 For <u>the word of God</u> is quick [living], and powerful, and sharper than any two-edged sword, piercing even to the dividing asunder of soul and spirit, and of the joints and marrow, and is a discerner of the thoughts and intents of the heart.

We see that *the sword of the Spirit* is *the Word of God*. Let's look at an example of how the *Word of God* can be used as a defensive weapon. This might surprise you, but Jesus Christ provides us with the best example on how to use *the Sword of the Spirit!* Following His baptism, Jesus was "led up of the Spirit into the wilderness to be tempted of [tested by] the devil" (Matt. 4:1). Who knows God's Word better than God Himself! Paul's prayed for the Ephesians to be filled with the knowledge of His Word. Jesus, as a man, stood firmly on the *Word of God* and see what happened.

In the following verses, Jesus provides us with three examples of how to use the *Word of God* as our defense against Satan's attacks. Luke 4:1-12:

> 1 **And Jesus being full of the Holy Ghost returned from Jordan, and was led by the Spirit into the wilderness, 2 Being forty days tempted of the devil. And in those days he did eat nothing: and when they were ended, he afterward hungered.**
>
> 3 **And the devil said unto him, If thou be the Son of God, command this stone that it be made bread. 4 And <u>Jesus answered him, saying, It is written, That</u>**

man shall not live by bread alone, but by every word of God.

5 And the devil, taking him up into an high mountain, shewed unto him all the kingdoms of the world in a moment of time. 6 And the devil said unto him, All this power will I give thee, and the glory of them: for that is delivered unto me; and to whomsoever I will I give it. 7 If thou therefore wilt worship me, all shall be thine.

8 And Jesus answered and said unto him, Get thee behind me, Satan: for it is written, Thou shalt worship the Lord thy God, and him only shalt thou serve.

9 And he brought him to Jerusalem, and set him on a pinnacle of the temple, and said unto him, If thou be the Son of God, cast thyself down from hence: 10 For it is written, He shall give his angels charge over thee, to keep thee: 11 And in their hands they shall bear thee up, lest at any time thou dash thy foot against a stone.

12 And Jesus answering said unto him,

It is said, Thou shalt not tempt the Lord thy God.

Look at the confrontation or challenges Satan posed to Jesus. Did He strike him with a sword? Cut off a limb? Pierce him or, in any way, attack him? Yet, notice the results of Jesus' use of Scripture. Satan departed from Him. Verse 13:

> 13 And when the devil had ended all the temptation, he departed from him for a season.

Jesus was a man at this time being tested in the wilderness. As the Son of God, He humbled Himself and became a man. Philippians 2:5-8:

> 5 Let this mind be in you, which was also in Christ Jesus: 6 Who, being in the form of God, thought it not robbery to be equal with God: 7 But made himself of no reputation, and took upon him the form of a servant, and was made in the likeness of men:
>
> 8 And being found in fashion as a man, he humbled himself, and became obedient unto death, even the death of the cross.

Until the Rapture, we are only human. It is God Who will do the fighting. Like Jesus, we are to use the *Word of God, the sword of the Spirit,* to thwart Satan who will then departed from us.

The more we know about the *Word of God,* the more we are in awe of His power. You might ask, "Why are Satan and his fallen angels afraid of *the sword of the Spirit?*" We find the answer in Revelation. Here is a passage written by the Apostle John exalting the Christ. Revelation 1:16-18:

> 16 **And he [Christ] had in his right hand seven stars: and out of his mouth went <u>a sharp two-edged sword</u>: and his countenance was as the sun shineth in his strength.**
>
> 17 **And when I saw him, I fell at his feet as dead. And he laid his right hand upon me, saying unto me, Fear not; I am the first and the last:**
>
> 18 **I am he that liveth, and was dead; and, behold, I am alive for evermore, Amen; and have the keys of hell and of death.**

As we draw closer to the end of Ephesians, we should think about our readiness for defense. Paul prayed to God the Father that we receive *the Spirit of wisdom and revelation in the knowledge of Him* (Eph. 1:17). Friend, that is knowledge of the Bible — God's Word! This knowledge is what will allow us to stand firm in our faith. No enemy, no way, no how can stand against *the sword of the Spirit!*

After Paul finishes describing what he calls *the armor of God,* he warns grace believers to pray and watch. Each soldier should maintain communication with headquarters especially while they are in the heat of a battle. We should remain connected to our glorious Head through prayer. Prayer is our direct link to the Living God. Ephesians 6:18:

> 18 **Praying always with all prayer and supplication in the Spirit, and watching thereunto with all perseverance and supplication for all saints;**

Our prayers or petitions should be for both us and for all saints. We must be watchful as we persevere together waiting for *His Calling* — the Rapture!

Paul asks the Ephesians to pray for him personally that he may be given the words to speak and that he may boldly make known the mystery of the Gospel of Grace — the same gospel by which we are saved. Verses 19-20:

19 And [pray also] for me, that utterance may be given unto me, that I may open my mouth boldly, to make known the mystery of the gospel, **20** For which I am an ambassador in bonds: that therein I may speak boldly, as I ought to speak.

He is finishing his letter to the Ephesians. As is usually the case, he will send the letter by the hand of a faithful brother. It was quite common to dispatch a letter to be delivered by a personal messenger. Tychicus was no doubt known by the grace believers in Ephesus. They would trust the letter he brought to them as being authentic. In addition to bringing the letter, he would also share with them other news about Paul's life and ministry. All this would be done to encourage them despite any hardships Paul was suffering. Verses 21-22:

21 But that ye also may know my affairs, *and* how I do, Tychicus, a beloved brother and faithful minister in the Lord, shall make known to you all things:

22 Whom I have sent unto you for the same purpose, that ye might know our affairs, and that he might comfort your hearts.

At the time of its writing, Paul was under house arrest in Rome. He will never again see his beloved Ephesians face to face. Following his pending trial in Rome, he will be put to death. During his later years, Paul's eyesight was deteriorating. So, he would dictate his letters to someone to write them on his behalf. Then, he would often sign them with his own hand as a means of authentication. Paul closes his letter to the Ephesians with the following blessing. Verses 23-24:

> 23 **Peace** *be* **to the brethren, and love with faith, from God the Father and the Lord Jesus Christ.** 24 **Grace** *be* **with all them that love our Lord Jesus Christ in sincerity. Amen.**

Paul ends this letter by including the same two words with which he opens his epistles. These are: *grace* and *peace*. For they comprise the complete message given to the Apostle Paul by the Risen Savior. It is though God's gracious act that we receive His gift of salvation by believing. By *grace* we are saved through faith. It puts an end to the enmity between God and those who accept. No longer are they enemies of God and subject to judgment. They now have *peace* with God through the righteousness of His Son. Amen!

Epilogue

Working through the book of Ephesians, I had some thoughts I would like to share. It concerns the world we live in and how the book of Ephesians is such an encouragement for those who await *His Calling.*

It is human nature for people to look at the world and think that it is worse now than ever before. It may appear that way, but that may not be the case. Evil has existed from the father of lies from the very beginning. Look at the book of Romans written by Paul about 57 A.D. In it, he summarizes the ungodliness of the world at that time. He wrote about those who chose not to know God. As you read this, remember this was written almost two thousand years ago. Romans 1:28-32:

> 28 And even as they did not like to retain God in their knowledge, God gave them over to a reprobate mind, to do

those things which are not convenient [suitable]; 29 Being filled with all unrighteousness, fornication, wickedness, covetousness, maliciousness; full of envy, murder, debate, deceit, malignity; whisperers, 30 Backbiters, haters of God, despiteful, proud, boasters, inventors of evil things, disobedient to parents,

31 Without understanding, covenantbreakers, without natural affection, implacable, unmerciful: 32 Who knowing the judgment of God, that they which commit such things are worthy of death, not only do the same, but have pleasure in them that do them.

Does this sound familiar? We have no further to look than a dozen or more popular news channels to confirm this.

Evil has not changed. It has become less hidden and more visible. No longer is there no shame in evil, but it is applauded. Do not be alarmed! Paul writes in Philippians 4:6-7:

6 Be careful [anxious] for nothing; but in every thing by prayer and supplication

**with thanksgiving let your requests be
made known unto God. 7 And the peace
of God, which passeth all understanding, shall keep your hearts and minds
through Christ Jesus.**

Here, we are talking about peace in an unpeaceful
world. Paul wrote about *the peace of God* that goes beyond our understanding. This is something that we
cannot understand because it goes beyond our ability, at present, to comprehend. This peace is seen
spiritually regardless of what is happening around
us.

This calm assurance comes from *the spirit of
wisdom and revelation in the knowledge of him*. It is
knowing what God said and believing it. It is about
understanding what God said and telling others.
This is evidence of believing and trusting in His
Word. As a result, we receive "the peace of God,
which passeth all understanding, shall keep your
hearts and minds through Christ Jesus" (v. 7).

We have everything we need because it has all
been provided for us. We are to hold fast to the truth
of God with our feet firmly planted. We should remember that we are children of God, members of His
household. Everything is going according to God's
plan. Continue in faith and studying the *Word of God*

as we wait for *His Calling* — the Rapture — our blessed hope!

Living *In Christ,*
Dr. David Alan Greene

Other GraceWord Publications

En español

Cartas A Teofilo
Efesios: Dispensacionalmente considerado
El evangelio Oculto: Una vez fue un misterio . . .

About The Author

Dr. David Alan Greene has over thirty-five years of experience as an insurance agent selling both property and casualty as well as life insurance. During his career, he taught and explained the content and meaning of policies to his clients. Now retired, he devotes much of his time to teaching the Bible.

He obtained his Bachelor of Theology, Master of Biblical Studies, and Ph.D. in Biblical Studies from Evangelical Theological Seminary where he holds the position of Dean of Graduate Studies. He also holds a Ph.D. in Christian Counseling. He has written numerous biblical commentaries and books on rightly dividing the Word of Truth.

www.ingramcontent.com/pod-product-compliance
Lightning Source LLC
Chambersburg PA
CBHW070749120626
46557CB00002B/518